# WHEN AID IS NO HELP

D1159407

*Promises, promises . . . This one, pictured in Cameroon, seems to head over some tough ground. Aid promises much, but getting it to the poorest is tougher than is usually realized.*

# When Aid is No Help

*How projects fail, and how
they could succeed*

JOHN MADELEY

with MARK ROBINSON, PAUL MOSLEY,
RUDRA PRASAD DAHAL, PRAMIT CHAUDHURI
and ANTONY ELLMAN

Intermediate Technology Publications 1991

Intermediate Technology Publications
103–105 Southampton Row, London WC1B 4HH, UK

© Intermediate Technology Publications 1991

A CIP catalogue record for this book is available from the
British Library.

ISBN 1 85339 077 1

Typeset by Inforum Typesetting, Portsmouth
Printed by BPCC Wheatons, Exeter

# Contents

Foreword

# ACRONYMS

| | |
|---|---|
| ACCORD | Agency for Co-operation and Research in Development |
| ASARRD | Asian Survey on Agrarian Reform and Rural Development |
| ADB(N) | Agricultural Development Bank of Nepal |
| BADC | Bangladesh Agricultural Development Corporation |
| BNDA | Banque Nationale pour le Developpment Agricole |
| BRDB | Bangladesh Rural Development Board |
| CIDA | Canadian International Development Agency |
| CMDT | Malian Company for Textile Development |
| DANIDA | Danish International Development Agency |
| DTWs | Deep tubewells |
| FAO | Food and Agriculture Organization of the United Nations |
| FRG | Federal Republic of Germany |
| GO | Group Organizer/Action Research Fellow (in Nepal) |
| HYVs | High-yielding varieties |
| IBFEP | Indo-British Fertilizer Education Project |
| ICAR | International Conference (of the United Nations) on Assistance to Refugees in Africa |
| ICDS | Integrated Child Development Services Programme (of India) |
| IFAD | International Fund for Agricultural Development |
| IFPRI | International Food Policy Research Institute |
| IRDP | Integrated Rural Development Programme (of India) |
| ILO | International Labour Organization |
| ITDG | Intermediate Technology Development Group |
| JFS | Joint Funding Scheme |
| LISP | Local Initiatives Support Project |
| MYRADA | Mysore Relief and Development Agency |
| NABARD | National Bank for Agricultural and Rural Development (of India) |
| NGO | Non-governmental organization |
| ODA | Overseas Development Administration |
| OPEC | Organization of Petroleum Exporting Countries |
| RIC | Rural Improvement Clubs (of the Philippines) |
| RPP | Rural Poor Programme (of Bangladesh) |
| SFDP | Small Farmer Development Programme (of Nepal) |
| UNHCR | United Nations High Commissioner for Refugees |
| UNIFEM | United Nations Development Fund for Women |
| VDFP | Village Development Fund Project (of Mali) |
| WFC | World Food Council |
| WHO | World Health Organization |

## NOTE

Please note: both hectares and acres are used as measurements of land size, according to which measure is used in the project area.

1 hectare = 2.471 acres.
1 acre    = 0.4047 hectares

# Foreword

*Do not be surprised when you see that the government oppresses the poor
and denies them justice and their rights.*

Ecclesiastes 5:8

THE ORIGINS OF this book date back to a hot day in Mali
during late March 1985. I had just visited a village called
Djiguiyara near the town of San in the east of the country. I
was there to look at a US $84 million rural development
project, Mali Sud, funded by the French and Dutch governments, the World Bank and the International Fund for Agricultural Development (IFAD). The project's aims were
laudable. They included the provision of credit to small-scale
farmers so that they could buy supplies, such as seeds and
tools, increase their output of food and so raise living standards in what is one of the world's poorest countries.

Djiguiyara is, in any terms, a resource-poor village. With
around 500 millimetres of rain a year the villagers grow only
millet and nuts. And they were suffering from the aftermath
of the African famine of 1984. I could see for myself on that
March day that food stocks were desperately low. Yet there
was no prospect of another harvest until September, and
even that was uncertain because the people had little money
to buy seeds for planting. Many were selling cattle and tools
in a desperate bid to survive.

Money in the village was chronically short. The villagers
told me that their community water pump had broken down
three weeks before. It had stayed unrepaired because they
did not have the money to put it right. The cost of the repair
was CFAfr3000 (around £6).

The 200 villagers were among the 30 million Africans
whose lives were then threatened by famine. Most, if not all,
could be numbered among the poorest of the poor. But
Djiguiyara was slap bang in the middle of the Mali Sud pro-

ject area. What help were the people getting, I asked project officials? 'None', was the reply, 'the village does not qualify.'

To say I was stunned was putting it mildly. This was, surely, exactly the kind of village that needed help. What was the point in having a multi-million pound internationally funded rural development project if the people most in need were not included? Why didn't the village qualify, I asked?

The project works through officially formed Village Associations, I was told. Only villages with a recognized association qualified. Such villagers were considered a reasonable economic bet: although they were poor they were rich enough to have some assets and could offer some guarantee that the money they borrowed they would repay. Again, villages that were judged by project managers to have a reasonable hope of forming an association also received assistance. If people could not organize in such a way, they did not qualify; the project did not give aid directly to individuals.

But what was clear from visiting other villages is that Village Associations existed in the better-off villages – better off not only in material terms, but where there was more motivation and commitment. Villages where people were poor and disorganized were excluded. They were considered too risky for credit.

Some 3500 villages made up the Mali Sud project area, and officials admitted that 15–20 per cent (at least 500) of them did not have an association and it was considered they had no chance of forming one. These villages were overwhelmingly the poorest.

What infuriated me that day as I left Djiguiyara, remembering the sunken eyes of young children abandoned by the world aid effort, was that the needs of those villagers ran a poor second to economic return. An aid project that was supposed to help the poor was excluding the poorest. Five hundred villages in just one area of one country had been left out. I considered this an outrage.

Later I heard that a local church was organizing to help people in excluded villages. That help could have made all the difference between life and death for many people but it did not alter the fact that the poorest were left to rely on charity.

The Mali Sud project is sadly no exception. For the past five years I have watched and noted the effects of official aid on the poorest. The only conclusion I can reach is that such aid only rarely gets through to them; that even those agencies that are trying hard to get aid through to the poorest are, in the main, not succeeding. There are exceptions, but they are few in number. Aid will not reach the poorest unless the reasons why existing projects are failing to reach them are analysed in a constructive way. It is in this spirit that this book is written. It comes about because of a gap in the literature concerning the failure of official, government-to-government aid. Roger Riddell, in *Foreign Aid Reconsidered*, says that for many donor countries, issues such as this are seen as complex and have either been 'avoided or else not yet answered'.[1]

In *Does Aid Work*? Robert Cassen points out that the debate on whether channelling aid through projects gets it effectively to poor people is 'among the weaker parts of evaluation work'.[2] The book devotes little more than 5 out of 400 pages to considering 'aid and poverty' and gives scant attention to what, in human terms, might reasonably be considered the major question: 'Does aid work for the poorest?'

Here I want to concentrate on official aid projects which are designed to benefit the poorest. The book tries to show why most of these projects are not achieving their aims, but it looks too at those which are having success, examining what is going right as well as wrong. It is about *appropriate* aid: it looks at questions such as: What is the most appropriate form of official aid for the poorest? How can official aid change and become more appropriate? How can the technology of aid-giving undergo radical reform to benefit those who need it the most?

I write as someone who is critical of most official aid to date but who is nonetheless in favour of materially wealthy nations sharing their wealth with poorer nations. I am, in short, friend not foe of development aid, but friend of what it could be rather than what it is in 1990. There are some glimmers of hope.

By facing up to the questions, pinpointing what is going wrong and identifying the obstacles that stand in the way of the poorest receiving aid, and also looking at projects which are working well, the book will, I hope, contribute to a better understanding of the issues and help towards removing the obstacles that stand in the way of getting aid to the poorest. Often it is only when we get down to the fine print of poverty-focused aid projects that we see the reasons why projects that are supposed to benefit the poorest are not doing so.

The challenge facing official aid is to be sensitive enough not to make the lot of the poorest harder, and to prove that it can actually get aid to them. If official aid can demonstrate this, it would earn far more friends in Western countries. It would be making a contribution that would be seen to be of clear value. 'Large parts of concerned public opinion want foreign assistance to be used primarily for helping the poorest people in developing countries', said the 1985 report of the Organization for Economic Co-operation and Development (OECD).[3] If official aid can change to reach the poorest, it would be seen by the general public to be meeting real needs, making a contribution of considerable value, helping to free people from poverty. Support for 'aid that works' would grow. It is my hope that this book will encourage governments to take more concerted action on behalf of the poor. Governments do not have to oppress the poor and deny them justice and their rights.

Part 1 is an overview of aid and the poorest; Part 2 presents case studies of how aid is failing to reach them. The rather shorter Part 3 looks at examples of how aid is reaching some of the poorest in Asia and Africa, and at the contribution of NGOS. I am aware that amid the failures in Part 2 there are elements of success, some of them promising. Also, that in the successes of Part 3 there are still aspects which are less than satisfactory. It is my own judgement that the projects in Part 3 have learned from mistakes and are painstakingly on the right lines. By contrast, the projects in Part 2 have some way still to go.

As Chapter 1 points out, around 500 million people lack basic necessities and can reasonably be described as the world's poorest. Most of the aid projects aimed at the poorest are targeted at this group. Within this 500 million category, however, there are wide income differentials, with the bottom half much poorer than the top half. This book is concerned with all 500 million but, wherever possible, particularly with the poorer half. All divisions of the poorest are arbitrary — ultimately you could divide down the poorest until you reach the poorest woman or man alive! The poorest 10 per cent of humanity, especially the poorest 5 per cent, seem reasonable percentages to take.

The main part of Chapter 1 looks at the record of official aid to date; Pramit Chaudhuri then outlines ways in which aid can reach the poorest. He says we should not expect too much 'from a small volume of aid facing a very large number of people in poverty'. Nonetheless something should be expected from aid. And whilst aid may only be able to help 'at the margin', the margin can be considerable. The right kind of aid can be a stimulus, a morale booster that can help the poorest out of the vicious circle of poverty.

IFAD was set up in 1977 to get aid through to the poorest. It has done some excellent work and has had a good press. Journalists who have seen IFAD projects have generally given them the benefit of any doubts they had. But IFAD's record is chequered. This book contains perhaps the first detailed criticism that has been made of the fund's work. Chapter 3 examines two IFAD projects in Mali that are flawed and looks at why.

India is the world's largest recipient of aid and the country has a government that is more committed than many to helping the poor. Chapter 4 looks at why most aid to India has not helped the poorest. Mark Robinson considers UK aid to Bangladesh in Chapter 5, and Paul Mosley and R. Prasad Dahal detail in Chapter 6 the problems of a project in Nepal designed to benefit small, poor farmers. Chapter 7 looks at how a project designed to help low-income women in the Philippines is missing the poorest.

Some things are going right with aid to the poorest and chapters 8 and 9 look at successful projects in Africa and Asia. Whilst it is true that aid is marginal to people's efforts, it can make the all-important difference. Aid can be a vital first step on the ladder out of poverty, as witness the people who have benefited under the Grameen Bank project. But even amid the successes there are often notes of caution to be struck, as these chapters show.

Non-governmental organizations have proved they can get help through to at least some of the poorest. They clearly make a valuble contribution, and could do more to help official aid to be more effective. This is considered in Chapter 10. The poorest are often disorganized, but are they passive creatures who are *unable* to organize? 'The passivity of the destitute exists only in the minds of those who dominate them', says Bernard Lecomte.[4] Helping the poorest to organize so that they can benefit from aid projects is examined in Chapter 10 by Antony Ellman.

Finally, the book asks what are the lessons of experience and draws conclusions as to how official aid needs to change to help the poorest.

This book is critical of certain IFAD and United Nations Development Fund for Women (UNIFEM) projects, but I hope it is critical in a positive way. And I want to stress that it would not have been written unless these agencies had helped me to see their projects. So my thanks are due to IFAD, The International Labour Organization (ILO) and UNIFEM for making possible visits to many of the projects described. In particular I want to thank Sergio Apollonio, formerly director of IFAD's information department and his colleagues Leonilda Garafola and Diedre Timpson-White; IFAD officials in Rome, too numerous to mention, Debbie Czeglady and Marilyn Carr of UNIFEM and Azita Berar of ILO. Also officials of the Mali Sud Rural Development Project, the Mali Village Development Project, the Local Initiatives Support Project in Lesotho, the Flour Milling Project in Gambia, the Rootcrops Project in the Philippines and the Revolving Fund for Refugees Project in Sudan. In particular, my special thanks are due to Pramit Chaudhuri, Mark Robinson, Paul Mosley, R. Prasad Dahal and Antony Ellman for their contributions to the book.

I am aware that it is not easy for an outsider paying a comparatively short visit to projects which are often quite complex to get a full picture of what is going on. Differences in languages do not help — the views of local people usually have to be translated. And people may be reluctant to speak out when project officials are present. I have always asked that officials show me and tell me of the not-so-good side of their projects as well as the good; most have been willing to do so. But I accept that there are difficulties in this area. What I have tried to do is to keep to the main issue and ask the fundamental question as to whether the poorest were gaining any benefit from the project I was seeing.

In addition to project officials, my thanks are due to the library staff at IFAD's library in Rome, the Institute of Development Studies library at Sussex University and the Overseas Development Institute library in London. My thanks to Alison and Sharon for their invaluable help. Needless to say, any mistakes are mine entirely.

*John Madeley*
*October 1990*

# PART 1: *The Problem*

# 1 Introduction

*Everyone seems desperately poor — even the relatively rich families.*

Good Aid[1]

If the global aid effort could be harnessed for the needy in an effective way it could play a significant role in helping to reduce poverty. In 1988 the 18 Western nations who belong to the Development Assistance Committee of the Organization for Economic Co-operation and Development (OECD) gave developing countries US\$48.1 billion in development aid; the Arab countries gave US\$2.7 billion and eastern European countries US\$4.7 billion; developing countries themselves contributed US\$0.45 billion. The overall level of aid was therefore around US\$56 billion.[2]

To many people the whole point of aid is to help the people who most need it. Yet that is far from the present position. 'The worst forms of poverty are not being dealt with', says Peter Peek.[3] He cites the Maharastra Employment Guarantee Scheme in India. Farmers owning over 25 acres (14 per cent of landowners) had a 32 per cent share of the area which benefited by the scheme; those owning less than 5 acres (35 per cent of landowners) had only 9 per cent. 'Similarly in a small-farm credit programme in Southern Darfur (Sudan) the farmers who took advantage of the scheme had average incomes substantially higher than those who did not.' Can official aid change so that it does help those who are most in need?

Whilst the need to target help to the very poorest is obvious, it is of course 'not always easy', in the words of the International Fund for Agricultural Development's (IFAD) 1987 Annual Report.[4] To make assistance available to all the poorest is far harder than is often recognized; it is probably the most immense task and the biggest challenge facing the aid effort today. There are sizable obstacles. Difficulties and

1

complexities are involved but are not impossible to overcome.

## Who are they and how many?

Who are the poorest? They are people who are 'often likely to be sick or malnourished, with few assets and large families . . . inarticulate, uneducated, unorganized, isolated and non-mobile', says Robert Chambers.[5] Hunger is likely to be their daily lot. They are chiefly to be found across Africa, Asia and Latin America, mostly in rural areas, although a growing number are crowded into Third World towns and cities.

Many of the poorest are effectively disenfranchised. They may have no vote, no organization, no influence. Appearing to have no power, they can safely be ignored by their own government and politicians. How can they be defined? One way is to take the number of people in the world whose incomes are below an officially recognized poverty line. In India alone this was estimated to be 275 million people in 1984–5, 222 million of whom live in rural areas.

Michael Lipton provides a working definition of the ultra-poor as those who spend virtually all their income on food yet cannot afford adequate calorific intake.[6]

How many are there? In 1988 world population stood at 5.128 billion.[7] According to a report of the Food and Agriculture Organization (FAO) of the United Nations, *Agriculture: Toward 2000*, the number of seriously undernourished people in the world, that is those with food intakes less than 40 per cent above the minimum base rate of 1520 calories a day, is 510 million.[8]

The study paints a stark picture. It says that between 1980 and 1985, food availability per head declined in 37 of 94 developing countries. Twenty-four of the 37 were African, with the effects of drought and deterioration of agricultural conditions further reducing consumption. But the crisis is wider. The economic crises of the 1980s have virtually halted 'the rising trend of calorific consumption in Latin America', says the study. And whilst some parts of Asia have made rapid strides in the past 30 years, it is still home to 'more than half the total poor in all developing countries'.

The hunger and gross poverty for over 500 million people in a world that has enough food for everyone is a continuing

2

scandal. Usually these people have few resources and very little to trade with the outside world. If they farm, they are subsistence farmers rather than cash-crop growers. It appears that around one in ten of the world's population can neither grow enough food nor afford to buy enough food for their proper nourishment. If their countries secured a better deal from world trade it might benefit them indirectly. Fairer trade is needed but it can be a blunt weapon for the poorest. Aid of the right kind can be far more important.

Definitions of the poorest are inevitably unsatisfactory. There is insufficient data, for example, to tell us who the poorest are *within families*. Inequality between the sexes is severe in some countries. Women often have less to eat than men, girls less than boys. A United Nations Children's Fund (UNICEF) survey of a community in western Mali found that 83 out of 412 children were not getting enough to eat and that most of them were girls. 'This is typical; we find it everywhere', said UNICEF country representative Tim Stone, 'malnutrition among girls is around twice as high as it is among boys.'[9]

Identifying who and where the poorest are is difficult, as Geoffrey Griffith highlights.[10] But we do know that the poorest often have insufficient land to grow food and can go hungry even when there is food in the market place. Robert Chambers writes of women in Sri Lanka who had not eaten for three days even though there was food in nearby shops.[11] Even at the height of the Ethiopian famine in 1984, aid workers were reporting that food was available close to stricken areas.

The World Health Organization (WHO) estimates that 20 per cent of the world's population, that is 1000 million people, are diseased, in poor health or malnourished. If we just take the worst-affected half of this group, we come again to around 500 million people who are often likely to be ill and hungry and who could reasonably be called 'the world's poorest'. Robert Cassen says there is no evidence to indicate that the bottom 10 per cent of income groups have been affected, either negatively or positively, by development projects.[12] In other words, the poorest 10 per cent gained nothing — but they did not have much to lose!

Reviewing Western aid to Bangladesh, a Chr. Michelsen Institute report has this to say:

the benefits of aid have gone almost exclusively to a small minority of people well placed to exploit the opportunities it has created. This picture of aid as primarily benefiting the 'haves' . . . is also valid for Norwegian bilaterial aid.[13]

Is official aid designed to benefit the poorest *peoples*? In a section called 'Why aid?' the Pearson Report, *Partners in Development*, said in 1969 that the objective of cooperation for international development

> . . . is to help poorer countries move forward, in their own way, into the industrial and technological age so that the world will not become more and more starkly divided into the haves and have-nots, the privileged and the less privileged.[14]

The use of the phrase 'poorer countries' means that the report was talking chiefly about have and have-not *countries* rather than *peoples*. This was an accurate reflection of the way Western donor nations viewed development assistance at that time.

Helping countries to raise their overall level of economic development was the primary aim. Countries first, and the people of those countries only indirectly, was the hallmark of bilateral (country-to-country) aid. And in the 1960s, even the neediest countries were often losing out.

A significant proportion of British aid goes to Commonwealth countries. 'But within the Commonwealth', wrote Judith Hart in 1973, 'there has been no logical distribution of aid according to the criteria of need'.[15] But the fundamental problem with Western donor nation bilateral aid programmes was that although they helped economic development in some countries, the benefits of a higher level of development were not 'trickling down' to the poorest. They remained little touched by the international aid effort. So donor governments began to think again.

A 1975 British government White Paper, 'Overseas Development, the Changing Emphasis in British Aid Policies: More Help for the Poorest', seemed to highlight an important shift of emphasis.[16] British government aid, said the White Paper, would

> give an increasing emphasis towards the poorest countries [and, furthermore] the government accepts that more should be done to ensure that a higher proportion of British aid should directly benefit not only the poorest countries *but the poorest people in those countries*.' (author's italics).

4

The White Paper went on to say that as many of the poorest lived in rural areas, the new emphasis meant giving more aid to rural development projects. But the strategy failed to herald any major shift and was short-lived. In 1980 the new Conservative Government said that, in future, greater weight would be given to financial, business and commercial considerations. Two years later an independent report concluded that the overwhelming majority of British aid was failing to reach the poor.[17]

Among other donor countries, aid for the poorest was also observed more in words rather than in practice. Paul Mosley notes that Denmark stressed its intention as early as 1972 'to reach the poorest part of the population'.[18] Yet, Denmark's aid agency, DANIDA, he points out, is 'hyper-sensitive to the risk of appearing to impose its own priorities on recipient governments . . . no references to a poverty strategy are made explicitly in negotiations with those governments'.

A 1984–5 Norwegian government White Paper refers to the objective of aid as contributing to the creation of lasting improvements in economic, social and political conditions for the people in developing countries.[19] At least this talks about people rather than just countries but it does not go so far as to refer to the *poorest* people.

The Dutch government decided to concentrate its aid on countries that were trying, in its judgement, to spread the benefits of development. Yet as Mosley points out, the countries chosen 'might not correspond to every observer's list of the most equitable governments'.[20]

## Is multilateralism the answer?

The world's largest multilateral aid agency (multilateral aid is that given through international bodies, such as the UN), the World Bank, makes a great deal of its 'poverty-oriented' strategy. 'The central goal of the World Bank is the reduction of poverty;', says the bank's 1988 Annual Report.[21] This is, at best, a misleading half-truth. Peter Peek points out that the projects supported by the World Bank are largely aimed at the better-off poor; the poorest 20 per cent scarcely get a look in.[22]

The bank's anti-poverty rhetoric can easily convey the impression that is talking about the very poor. At worst, the bank is misleading the international community about what it is achieving. Maybe its projects are helping to reduce poverty, although this is doubtful, but there is little or no evidence that its projects are reducing the worst poverty. In some cases they serve only to reinforce it.

The snag is that the World Bank acts like a bank rather than an aid agency. It talks and understands the language of finance, not that of the poor. The World Bank's bottom line is that of banks the world over — profit, return on capital employed, rather than human need. Its commitment to 'the neo-classical theory of full-cost recovery' from its poverty projects makes impeccable sense for a bank.[23] But not for an aid agency that is sincere about wanting to reach the needy.

Having seen the World Bank in action in a number of countries, my own view is that its officials rarely understand the problems and aspirations of the poor. I have met its country representatives in some of the world's poorest countries who have shown what can only be called an arrogant insensitivity to the needs of the poorest. The development projects drawn up and implemented in a World Bank office are usually poles apart from local realities. But then the world of a bank is so very different from the world of the needy.

An international bank is hardly a suitable vehicle for getting aid through to the very poor. If the international community really cares about the poorest, then some fundamental questions need to be asked about why it continues to allow a bank to act as the largest multilateral aid agency.

Mindful of the slowness of change in international bodies, the reality is that the World Bank may be around for some time yet. If it is to make a start serving the very poor it needs, at the very least, to examine its own rhetoric and, instead of being carried away by its own claim to be reducing poverty, to stop and look at the evidence. The World Bank is not the only aid agency that has failed to reach the poorest. In the official aid effort overall, 'people' have run far behind finance, allowing little scope for the genuine participation of the poor.

Bernard Lecomte notes:

Financiers claim to be realists; before spending money they need to know what the proposed project will do, who is to carry it through, who is to benefit . . . and so on. And when the project

6

duly funded reaches the field, its promoters will look for the local people's backing and participation. Yet taking part in something decided in advance, and out of their hands, is seen as insulting to community leaders.[24]

Village chiefs in West Africa told him of their experience with an aid project — 'they never came to ask our opinions to suggest something that we can organise for ourselves'. Projects like that do not allow for the participation of any local people, let alone the poorest.

As far back as 1974 the need for a different kind of organization was recognized at a major international food conference in Rome. The world's governments picked up a suggestion which the then United States Secretary of State, Henry Kissinger, and the Shah of Iran had put to the conference and resolved unanimously to take action to ensure that 'within a decade, no child will go to bed hungry, no family will fear for its next day's bread, no human being's future and capacities will be stunted by malnutrition'.

Having said that, donor governments realized that they had to do something about it. The aid effort, as it was then constructed, was clearly not going to play much of a part in bringing it about. So two new multilateral organizations were set up, the World Food Council (WFC) and IFAD.

The WFC's task is to help Third World governments formulate policies to increase food output. In practice the WFC has had an uneasy relationship with the longer established FAO and its potential has scarcely been realized.

It seemed that IFAD was an organization that could break through the log-jam and get aid to the poorest. This had to happen if the 1974 conference resolution was to get anywhere. As Chapter 2 shows, the agency which started off with brave hopes and has had successes, has been scandalously underfunded by the very governments that brought it into being. As such it has not made the contribution it might have done towards the realization of the aims of the 1974 conference. But what IFAD has done is genuinely to try to get aid to the poorest. It has sometimes failed, but there are valuable lessons in the failures. In IFAD's work the problems can be seen more clearly and identified.

In 1984, the 'decade to end hunger' was over. A 1984 UNICEF report made sad reading: 'Tonight more children will go to bed hungry, their capacities stunted, than on the night in 1974 when those words [about ending hunger] were spoken'.[25]


## Non-project aid

Most official aid, bilateral and multilateral, is given to specific development projects. But non-project aid increased in the later half of the 1980s, amounting in 1989, for example, to 16 per cent of the World Bank's total aid. Does part of the answer to getting aid to the poorest lie in more non-project aid so that recipient countries can use the money as they wish for the relief of the worst poverty?

Much of the increase in non-project aid has come in the form of finance for developing countries to undertake programmes of 'structural adjustment'. (adjusting the structure of an economy to try to make it more efficient). Such programmes often meant cutting government services such as health and education and reducing subsidies. The losers were inevitably the poorest. For them, structural-adjustment aid proved a hideous distortion of the kind of aid they needed.

There is an old but now largely discredited argument that the poor have a better chance of being made stronger under circumstances of economic growth. To rely on the benefits of growth trickling down to the poorest is now seen to represent the triumph of hope over experience.

Aid given without strings for overall programmes of development (so-called programme aid) has the potential to help the poorest — although its line to them may be long and wear thin before it reaches them. Cassen argues that although the poorest 10 per cent may not have gained much from many projects 'in terms of income or productive assets, they do appear to have gained indirectly from those projects which have cheapened their food . . . and from a large number of projects in the welfare sectors'.[26] In a study of projects supported by the British Government in Cajamarca, Peru, Mosley takes the view, however, that if the poorest are to be  reached, 'it must be done directly and not by hoping for indirect spinoff'.[27]

Neither project nor programme aid can reach the poorest if recipient governments do not want to let it reach them. There is a link between poverty and unrepresentative government. No aid can get to the poorest in countries where government policies and development projects show no interest in allowing any such thing, no interest in representing their needs. Political commitment to reaching them is essential but often lacking. Donors may not be asked to back projects that help the poorest. There is some truth in the statement 'If the poor stay poor in developing countries it will often be because the less poor in those countries want it that way.'[28]

Whilst this does pose a problem, donors are not powerless. They can let it be known that requests for projects which genuinely help the poorest will be considered sympathetically and even given priority. What is clear is that if the will of Third World governments to reach the poorest exists, the money is often lacking; it is this that links aid for the poorest very firmly with the global economy.

If the governments of countries receiving aid *want* to help official aid reach the poorest, there are certain changes they could make: land reform schemes are highly beneficial; minimum-wage legislation helps; subsidies for the poorest are an option although not always administratively easy to organize; the provision of health-care services has proved to be of benefit — when sickness among the very poor has been reduced, incomes have often risen because they are able to spend more of their time at work; 'a good programme of agricultural research and extension', is listed by Albert Berry of the University of Toronto as among measures that could help; also 'good prices for relevant farm products, primary education, rural roads, a progressive tax system'.[29]

## Harming the poorest

In some instances, official aid directly harms the poorest. By helping the slightly less poor at the expense of the poorest, it can widen rural inequalities. Projects to help women, who are usually poorer than men, have ended up strengthening the men not the women! An IFAD-funded rice project in Gambia, the Jahally-Pacharr, was intended to help poorer women to farm rice on their own land. But there is no tradition of women owning land in Gambia, a problem that was not faced before the project started. As a result it was the generally better-off *men* who kept the land, could afford the supplies for agriculture and who reaped the project's benefits. 'Despite considerable efforts by program planners to

9

maintain women's access to the new rice technologies, women farmers ended up mainly with access to lower-level, lower-yielding rice technologies', said one report.[30]

Large hydro-electric schemes, 'official aid' agency favourites, which flood people out of their homes benefit the better-off who can afford the electricity the schemes generate but can be a disaster for the poorest.

Frequently the poorest have been treated as disposable pawns in grandiose schemes. There are all too many examples of this. In Sri Lanka I have seen 45 000 people forced out of their homes through the building of the Victoria Dam, Britain's biggest-ever aid project it was claimed at the time. People were removed from towns and villages where they had lived all their lives so that the area could be flooded under a scheme that would provide electricity to industry — but not to the people flooded out. The people were never consulted about the dam; they were told only it was coming. Mournful dawn convoys of people were to be seen in and around the town of Teldeniya, the heart of the new reservoir. They left behind fertile land which enabled them to survive and were taken inland to an area of jungle country where they had to prepare new land themselves, often with little or no tools or services. The pitiful compensation they received in no way made up for the heartbreak they suffered.

In Zambia's Gwembe Valley, a very poor community suffered when a hydro-electric barrage was built across the Zambesi River, creating the world's biggest man-made lake but leaving local people to farm a tiny strip of land at the lakeside, their good land submerged under the new water.

These are just two examples. Aid that is not aimed specifically at the poorest often ends up causing them harm.

## Aid and poverty†

PRAMIT CHAUDHURI

Much public support for aid comes from the belief that it helps the poor in the Third World. There have been few

† An adapted version, reprinted with permission from the *Bulletin of the Institute of Development Studies*, 1986, Vol. 17, No. 2.

attempts at systematic evaluation of the impact of aid projects on poverty. Aid can both help and hinder in reducing poverty. It can only do so, however, at the margin and always in the context of national policies and priorities, which it can influence positively or negatively but cannot override. In far too many developing countries, the poor have not been the primary beneficiaries of development. The limited impact of aid on poverty is part of that story.

Against the scale of needs, net aid, now and in the foreseeable future, is rather small for most countries with many poor people. The structural characteristics of poverty make it difficult for external resources or agencies to reach the poor, except in the context of a national policy that actively directs such a process.

In so far as aid can assist the relief of poverty, it can do so in four main ways:

○ By contributing to the overall growth of the economy, it can create the conditions for rising incomes and greater availability of the goods and services consumed by the poor.
○ By financing specific projects or sectoral outlays of particular relevance to the poor, it can help to raise directly the private consumption of the poor.
○ By investment in social infrastructure, it can channel income benefits to the poor, such as better education, health or family-planning facilties.
○ It can help to promote, or hold back, processes of social and institutional change that are likely to benefit the poor. Such changes are often essential for a redistribution of income-creating assets, such as agricultural land, to small peasants and other low-income households.

Some of the poorer countries, such as Sri Lanka, or some of the poorer relations in certain countries, such as Kerala in India, have managed to bring about substantial improvements to the welfare of the poorer sections of the population in terms of consumption, literacy or infant mortality, despite modest economic growth. Nevertheless, in the poorer, populous countries of South Asia, and in most African countries, the number of people living in absolute poverty has been rising.

The rural poor make up the bulk of people living in poverty in less developed countries (LDCs); therefore efforts to

11

reach the poor should be concentrated in rural areas. Most people work in agriculture, either as small peasants or agricultural labourers, and all of them spend a very large part of their incomes, say 60–70 per cent, on food products of agricultural origin.

Aid that increases the productivity of the poor peasants — better implements, minor irrigation, flood control or better rural roads providing access to markets — helps poverty and does not harm growth. Aid that destroys, or helps to destroy rural jobs, such as subsidized mechanization, harms the poor. Aid that is directed towards increasing food production helps the poor as consumers by improving availability and reducing prices and, in the longer run, by encouraging agricultural research *in situ*. The problem is that too little aid does that. Even without aid to agriculture, too much of the aid helps to spread labour-displacing technologies, to create a market for donor country exports. The most obvious example of such practices is probably the tractorization of farming in South Asia.

Poverty-oriented aid policies are less likely to be fruitful if pursued either within an inappropriate policy framework or a worsening economic climate. Donor countries share responsibilites for both, responsibilities that have not always been carried out wisely. Recessionary policies in the international economy can destroy export prospects for agricultural commodities in the short run and discourage investment in the long run in the export sector. Sudden decreases in (government) expenditure may shift the burden of the cuts disproportionately onto the poor.

The overall impression from the case studies that were carried out for *Does Aid Work?* was that donors had neither an overall strategy towards poverty-elimination nor did they pay adequate attention to the poverty-impact of aid-financed projects. On the recipient side, pricing policies, choice of technology, or ground rules determining access to scarce inputs such as credit, all militate against the poor benefiting from project expenditure.

However, there are some general principles, for don'ts, rather than do's. As yet we know far too little about the nature and workings of the various forms of leakages that deny the benefits of growth to the poor. There is no evidence of any inherent conflict between poverty-eradication and profitability.

12

The poor are most likely to benefit from projects that are directed exclusively towards them, such as employment opportunities for unskilled labour or increases in the supply of the cheaper food crops, such as millet or cassava, where it is more difficult for the better-off to hijack the benefits. The poor are least likely to benefit from large-scale, modern-sector projects; the indirect linkages are not strong enough. And, complicated, multi-objective, integrated rural development projects seldom produce the benefits they promise. Many countries do not have the administrative capacity or skill-infrastructure that is necessary for success.

It makes more sense to design projects with clear and simple objectives, such as improved irrigation facilities, that can be implemented and monitored. In choosing such projects one cannot assume simply that national policies interpret local needs correctly, for example irrigation policies in India and rural development policies in Tanzania. If the poor are to participate in, and benefit from, such projects, the techniques chosen have to be accessible to them in terms of resources, being simple, inexpensive in terms of input requirements, and low risk.

It is important to take account of locally available resources, and local agronomic conditions. Adaptability and flexibility towards local needs and resources and conditions are important attributes. Aid for tractors is a fairly clear case of aid that does not meet these criteria and that might make the poor worse off. Livestock distribution for the landless, where good quality, healthy cattle are not locally available is another. Lastly, the involvement and direct participation of the intended beneficiaries in project design and implementation is an important means of ensuring that benefits reach the target groups. It is quite often the case, however, that projects which benefit the poor, benefit the better-off even more, thus exacerbating rural inequality.

The impact that aid can make in the agricultural sector is critical to the well-being of the poor, both as producers and consumers. There is evidence that aid has been successful in this area by helping the poor as consumers, either by increasing the production of staple foodcrops or by increasing their availability to the poor. There is less evidence that aid has helped the poor as producers; it has not been particularly successful in redistributing productive assets to the poor. Aid has not worked miracles for large numbers, but it has made certain things possible, and some others less difficult, for significant numbers of the rural population, but only where national policies and priorities have not been pulling the other way.

Aid can help in three main ways:

○ It can provide resources such as rural credit or fertilizers, or it can operate capacity for producing inputs, for example by financing fertilizer factories or irrigation networks.

○ It can improve the distribution of a given volume of output over space or time through the creation of better storage facilities or rural transport networks. The technological requirements of such schemes are often locally available, labour-intensive inputs rather than expensive imported capital items such as tractors. In such cases, what is required is local-cost support, subject to two general provisos that apply to all aid resources: such support has to be for a clearly specified period, leading towards self-reliance; and its foreign-exchange component has to be valued at an appropriate shadow price.

○ In the longer term, it can assist in agricultural research, through technical and other means. The relationship between expenditure on agricultural research and its consequent benefits in the form of a higher, or a more stable, level of output is a complex one. It is undeniable, however, that such expenditure has led to very substantial increases in agricultural output in South Asia.

Many of the poor, whether very small cultivators or landless agricultural workers, are not buyers of food, which forms the largest item of their expenditure. An increase in the production of foodgrains helps the poor by improving supply and preventing too high prices, at least for large countries where domestic food prices are not determined by world food prices. The low priority given to agricultural research in sub-Saharan Africa, the low levels of government recurrent finance devoted to research expenditure, the lack of high-yielding varieties of root crops and the stagnation of agricultural production in the area stand in stark contrast to that experience.

In two articles in the 1970s, John Lewis stressed the case for public works as a poverty-eradication policy. They are one of the few direct means available to get to the rural poor, especially the landless poor. They can adopt flexible, labour-

14

intensive technologies, with a high ratio of wages to total costs, and can lead to the creation of useful rural assets. Such rural capital formation only helps the poor if the ownership vests in the poor through, say, community development or self-help schemes, or the assets provide continuous employment opportunities at above-subsistence wages. On the other side, many public works are 'non-viable make-work schemes', and make heavy demands on local administrative resources. Both wages and the assets they create can leak to better-off rural households, benefiting the landowning groups by raising land values.

Rural public works are not always effective at providing continuous employment to the poorest groups of the rural population, but can raise the incomes of parts of the lower income rural groups for significant parts of the year.

The success or otherwise of public-works schemes in lessening poverty depends critically on ensuring that the wages that are created can be spent effectively on locally available wage-goods, without greatly pushing up their prices. Schemes like poverty programmes are a roundabout means of increasing the essential consumption of the poor, especially food consumption. The question naturally arises: can aid not be used to increase directly that consumption by direct food transfers to the poor, through rationing or direct subsidies? In the context of aiding 'the poorest', it is by no means a rhetorical question as the poorest often cannot, for one reason or another, participate to any significant extent either in work or in benefits from asset ownership.

Other key factors required for the well-being of the poor are literacy and health. These social components of consumption are best provided, in poor LDCs, through public investment which in turn can be financed through aid. Primary literacy is important because it improves access to technology and resources. Female literacy helps additionally in improving intra-family distribution and child-care practices, and in reducing fertility.

The main social consumption components of improved health status are the availability of primary health care, pure water and improved sanitation. Such investment as is required is costly for poor countries, not because unit costs need to be high but because it requires a wide coverage of these facilities to make an appreciable impact on a large and dispersed population in rural areas. While the import-content of such investment is low, or ought to be low if appropriate modes of delivery are chosen, recurring local costs tend to be high.

There are certain things that donors can do, and just as important is what they can avoid doing. Technical assistance, local-cost support and improvements in local administrative structures are what is often required. What is often not required are imported capital inputs or, for example, urban hospitals. In the urban sector, improvement in public health facilities, water supply for the poorer areas, and 'site and service' schemes are all important examples of aid collaboration. That such collaboration can be effective in what might appear to be unfavourable environments is exemplified by the Calcutta Metropolitan Development Scheme. The problem is the replicability of such schemes, which depend on local skills and initiative, as well as on finance.

Aid is more likely to make a positive contribution to poverty-reduction where national priorities and policies are poverty oriented. The question arises whether donors can themselves influence those policies and priorities. The limited role of aid in bringing about institutional reform that would facilitate a firmer attack on poverty can be illustrated by two examples from within the sphere of agricultural policy: land reform and institution-building.

The role of donor policy in land reform is likely to be limited. The political and historical circumstances in which land reform was implemented in Taiwan or donor pressure exerted in South Korea are not replicable, though where national policy is geared to such an objective, aid can help in overcoming particular constraints. Years ago the World Bank laid down very specific guidelines for its lending policy, going so far as to exclude countries that were not willing to promote land-reform policies. Not surprisingly, perhaps, such sanctions are seldom implemented; nor is it clear that such action would be fruitful if it were to be another demonstration as donor power.

Too much has been claimed for aid by its supporters, and too much has been blamed on aid by its critics. Aid has in the past made little direct impact on poverty, not least because neither donors nor recipients had attempted seriously to channel aid and other resources towards the poor. Yet much can be learnt from the past experience about using scarce aid resources more effectively to make an impact on poverty.

# 2 The International Fund for Agricultural Development (IFAD)

*IFAD was created . . . to be different, to assist the rural poor by-passed by development efforts.*[1]

IT WAS PARTLY due to the failure of official aid to reach the very poorest peoples that IFAD was set up in November 1977 as a specialist agency of the United Nations. IFAD was one of two agencies, the other being the World Food Council, that came out of the food conference at Rome in 1974 (see page 9).

Governments committed themselves to take action to ensure that 'no family will fear for its next day's bread'. The aim was noble. It suggested an all-out attack would be made on the ancient enemy, hunger. IFAD was, it seemed, unique in that it was given the task of getting aid to the poorest of the poor, the people that other agencies were missing. Yet the following years witnessed governments failing to put their money where their mouths were. They underfunded IFAD from the start and then continued to cut its funds, reducing it to a pale shadow of the agency needed.

If governments did not really mean it in 1974, or maybe if they simply underestimated the nature of the effort needed to reach the poor, at least in IFAD they set up an agency which has made an attempt to reach the poorest and whose experience has helped to show more clearly what are the problems of doing so.

The stated objective of IFAD is:

> to mobilize additional resources to be made available on concessional terms for financing primarily projects specifically designed to improve food production systems, the nutritional level of the poorest populations in developing countries and the condition of their lives.[2]

The fund has a double 'uniqueness' — it is the only UN agency to be jointly funded both by Western countries and oil exporting countries which belong to the Organization of Petroleum Exporting Countries (OPEC).

Whilst this joint-funding arrangement was heralded as a breakthrough in 1984, involving the oil rich countries more closely in the aid effort, the funds were voluntary and had be replenished every three years. This was to cause seemingly endless problems. IFAD was given US$1 billion for the first three years of its work, from 1978 to 1980, with Western countries contributing 58 per cent of the total and OPEC 42 per cent. It was replenished on the same 58:42 basis for the 1981–3 period. Funds were then 'increased' to US$1.1 billion, which was in fact a cut as this figure did not keep pace with inflation. Sharper cuts were to follow.

During its first six years IFAD struggled to do things differently from existing aid agencies. It took a many-sided approach, based on the fact that the causes of hunger are complex and that, for everyone to have enough food, action is needed on a number of fronts. It is not enough, for example, just to increase food output; people go hungry, sometimes when food is plentiful, because they simply do not have the money to buy food. As most of the hungry live in the rural areas of the Third World this means that rural development and action to raise the incomes of the poorest were seen as essential.

Under the guidance of a Saudi Arabian President, Abdel M. Al-Sudeary, IFAD began giving loans to small farmers and the rural poor, usually by working through an official development agency in the aid-recipient country. Countries with a per capita income of less than US$300 in 1976 received interest-free loans, repayable after 50 years, with a grace period of 10 years. (A 1 per cent-a-year service charge was made.) Better-off countries had to repay within 15–20 years.

By the end of 1983 IFAD was funding 135 projects which, it claimed, would led to 20 million tons of additional food output. But the fund was constrained both by its lack of experience and by the demands of donor countries. It was new and many of its projects were mounted jointly with other agencies, such as the World Bank. Being new, it was uncertain of its ground and tended to be pushed around by the more experienced agencies. In the meantime, donor governments still expected it to show a good return on the aid funds

18

it was using, and the US, for one, seemed satisfied. In 1984 six US government teams carried out a survey of 19 IFAD-supported projects in 14 countries and seemed impressed by what members of one team called the agency's 'careful stewardship of resources'.[3]

In December 1983, however, Western and OPEC donor countries had a serious disagreement on how IFAD should be funded from 1984 to 1986, a disagreement which threatened its existence. The dispute was over whether the percentages the two sides contributed to IFAD's overall funding should change or stay the same. The OPEC group argued that their economies were much weaker in 1983 than in 1977 and that they could not afford to pay as much. The United States maintained that 'burden sharing' was a principle of IFAD and must continue roughly as before.

But it seemed that whatever the percentages, IFAD was going to receive less. In the United States the Reagan administration was not keen on multilateral aid agencies over which it had little control — a stance from which all the UN agencies suffered. OPEC indicated that if Western countries gave US$465m, then it would give US$295m. This made the overall total only US$760m for three years, a sharp drop on the 1981–3 period.

Although the OPEC offer would still mean that it contributed 39 per cent of IFAD's funds, the United States stuck by its insistence that OPEC pay a larger share. IFAD was stymied for a few percentage points. In 1984 IFAD was a fund with no funds, receiving no money for its work. It was a tragic irony that in the very week in October 1984 when the scale of the Ethiopian famine became known to millions, the IFAD Governing Council met in Paris to try to resolve the disagreement. It failed.

The leader of the US delegation, Richard Derham, said that IFAD was formed on the basis of 'equal participation of resources'. But OPEC group spokesman, Faisal A. Al-Khaled of Kuwait, pointed out that IFAD's constitution said nothing about burden-sharing and that countries should donate to the fund in accordance with their ability to do so.

IFAD's Algerian president-elect, Idriss Jazairy, asked how it could be explained

to the 500 million men and women whose survival is threatened by hunger and poverty that we cannot come to their aid because

19

of a disagreement on a matter of principle that concerns the provision of a few dozen million dollars.

It would be a scandal, said Jazairy, if IFAD were allowed to collapse at a time of such great need in the world. It was clear that the fund would run out of money by early 1985, causing lending to stop. IFAD was in danger of becoming the first UN agency to go out of business in the United Nations 40-year history. The tragedy of the disagreement was that the amount of money concerned was, relatively, tiny. Bula Hoyos of Colombia, held the United States 'solely responsible' for the breakdown of the talks in Paris, saying that IFAD was a victim of the US dislike of multilateral aid organizations.

Representatives of Western countries meanwhile waxed lyrical about IFAD's work. Richard Derham, for example, stressed that IFAD had done more than lend money: 'IFAD's contribution', he said, 'goes beyond its own undertaking; its influence on small farmer development has stimulated other bilateral and other multilateral programmes.' Britain's representative, Peter McLean, said that IFAD has been successful in persuading other development agencies to back the approach of helping the poor, 'and has built up a considerable body of knowledge about how this can be done'.

For IFAD to receive such limited support, when it was at least doing something to reach the poor, was bizarre. In 1985 the fund tottered on the brink of extinction, received nothing and lending little, a grim testimony to the failure of donor governments to fund an agency that was more urgently needed than ever. In January 1986 the issue was settled but only by a savage cutback in the level of funding. Donors agreed to give IFAD US$487m for its work over the 1985–7 period, Western countries pledging US$276m and OPEC US$184m, a 60:40 divide. The developing world itself contributed US$27m. In real terms, IFAD had little over a quarter of the funds it had had for its first three years. The lower level was offset a little by a decision to set up a Special Programme for Africa to help countries badly hit by drought and desertification.

Squabbling has continued to mar the fund. Only after more prolonged negotiations was the IFAD kitty replenished for the 1988–90 period with US$522m, again a cut in real terms compared with the previous three years.

Despite its limited budget, IFAD ended the 1980s in a more confident mood. 'IFAD's survival as an institution is no more an issue', Idriss Jazairy told the 1989 Governing Council. Lack of funds was still, however, a constraint. The British government representative, Ian Buist, told that same Governing Council that 'the fund cannot exploit more than a fraction of the opportunities that cry out for action'. But funding problems were to some extent offset by the fact that a number of IFAD's early loans were being repaid in the late 1980s, and repayments would flow more rapidly in the 1990s. This will enable the fund to move closer to being a self-funding organization.

## Achievements

It is IFAD's claim that its first ten years 'have confirmed that no people are too poor, too isolated or too marginalised to be beyond the reach of effective projects'.[4] It has impressive achievements to its credit. Between 1978 and 1989, IFAD loaned over US$2.9 billion to some 266 projects in 93 developing countries, loans which have attracted an additional US$8.2 billion from governments and other development organizations. Seeds, fertilizer, tools and low-interest credit found their way into the hands of farmers and landless people who had previously received little outside assistance. IFAD's estimates suggested that its projects would lead to an additional 24m tonnes of cereal being grown, helping 180m of the world's poor.

The agency claimed that it had exploded the myth that the poor are beyond reach and had increased understanding of how to help them. It has shown longer established development agencies, such as the World Bank, that helping the poor is an economic proposition, and that poor people are a largely untapped resource capable of producing a great deal more food and increasing their incomes if they get the right kind of help from outside. When, for example, the World Bank was asked to fund the Grameen Bank project in Bangladesh, it said no. Borrowers had no guarantees to offer. IFAD helped the World Bank to see that it is no use talking about helping the poor unless the poor are treated as trustworthy. It has helped in a small way to nudge the bank away from rigid criteria over lending to the very poorest in the developing world. Repayment rate on Grameen Bank's loans is over 98 per cent (see Chapter 8).

IFAD has funded the less fashionable agricultural research that tries to increase yields of those foods on which the poorest rely, has worked more closely with non-governmental organizations (NGOs) than other official aid agencies and has emphasized since the mid-1980s the way that poverty is damaging the environments of the poor, thus reinforcing their poverty. And it has had some notable successes with low-cost credit schemes. IFAD claims to be pursuing 'a new approach, stressing people's participation . . . it has sought to enlist the active participation of the beneficiaries in the projects it supported from the design stage onwards'.[5]

Richard Bissell, the US representative on the 1988 IFAD Governing Council, told the council that 'IFAD has reached the poor by consulting them first'. It is true that, especially as it gained in experience, IFAD has made a determined attempt to base its projects on what the poorest wanted. The IFAD-funded Local Initiatives Support Project (LISP) in Lesotho is an outstanding example of this (see Chapter 9).

And yet IFAD's rhetoric is overdone. IFAD glosses over some of the very real problems in reaching the poor and it is less than forthcoming about its own failures. Whilst it talks of involving the poorest at the design stage of a project, it does not say that such attempts have usually failed — because the poorest are usually not organized sufficiently to take part. The effective exclusion of the very poorest from two projects in Mali illustrates the problems (this is discussed in Chapter 3).

Poor people are often unable to organize themselves into groups that satisfy the world of official projects. They do not conform to what outsiders are looking for. The harsh experience of life of people who live in the poorest villages may have left them demoralized and perhaps apathetic about any structured plan. They may not want to do things the way outsiders think they should — which makes it risky for donors to support them.

And the poorest are usually reluctant to take risks: 'For very poor people', says Peter Evans, manager of LISP, 'the risk of getting involved in a project is too high. They are scared of loans, scared to work in groups.' The pilot scheme that LISP launched to overcome this difficulty has shown that there are ways round the problems. But they need careful, patient and painstaking attention to detail.

If there is an organizational problem getting aid through to the poorest, there are other obstacles too. Putting credit into the hands of resource-poor farmers, says IFAD, is one of the best ways of releasing their potential to grow more food. 'Well-designed credit programmes can play a major role in reaching the rural poor', says an IFAD study of 27 projects which are providing credit for the rural poor.[6]

The Grameen Bank project is an excellent example. But there are snags; in practice there are financial considerations that can exclude the poor. Any aid project wants to be successful. In the case of IFAD projects, there is a desire to help the poor and to prove that the poor are a good risk. The aim is laudable, especially as practically no other official development agency is doing it. Donor countries welcome the fact that the poor are being reached, but at the same time they want to see 'success' in terms of accountability and 'responsible' use of aid funds. Donor countries expect projects to be financially viable. This means that people who are judged to be risky, usually the poorest, are unlikely to receive loans. 'For aid agency decision makers, a "good" project is one that enables a particular goal to be achieved most expeditiously and reliably with lowest costs and highest returns', says Bernard Lecomte.[7]

Project managers on the ground have a legitimate concern to ensure that their project is a success. IFAD-supported projects will typically lend money at between 10 and 20 per cent annual rate of interest. Managers want to achieve maximum repayment rates, convincing their donors back in Western capital cities that they are worth backing. But this seems to require that agencies have to be careful about who receives loans. IFAD is often reluctant to admit publicly to these contraints, although IFAD officials do not hide them privately. But without open recognition of the problems, there is an air of unreality about the fund's operations, for millions of the very poor will stay beyond IFAD's reach.

In some IFAD-supported projects there has been a lack of sensitivity to the needs of the poorest which is disturbing — in the Village Development Fund Project (VDFP) in Mali, for example (see Chapter 3).

IFAD also indulges in too much hype over the amount of money it spends on administration. Its claim to be one of the most cost-effective UN agencies is reasonably sound. 'IFAD's cost effectiveness', says its 1983 Annual Report, 'is demonstrated by its average administrative costs in the past six years which have been less than 5 per cent of the amount of loans and grants approved each year.'[8] But this is a half-truth. The fund tends to overlook the amount of project money that is spent locally on administration and management. In some projects over a fifth of the money allocated to a project can go to cover local administrative costs. In the cast of the VDFP in Mali, for example, 19.6 per cent is spent on project management and control, monitoring and evaluation studies, and this does not seem to be an unusual percentage. If this project is typical, then IFAD does not spend 5 per cent on administration, monitoring, management and evaluation. The real figure, taking both head office and local spending into account, is around 25 per cent — and it could be much higher.

Such costs are nonetheless still low for an official development agency. But IFAD's strength in keeping administrative costs down is a weakness in that the fund does not have the money to have its own resident representatives on the ground in developing countries. In joint projects the bigger agencies, the ones who can afford to have people on the ground, tend to get their way.

How many of IFAD's projects are reaching the very poorest? Between 1985 and 1989 I visited ten of the fund's projects.[9] There is no doubt that the poor are being reached. But are they the poorest, the 'bottom 10 per cent', the people most at risk when famine looms? Some of the projects I have seen were impressive and in some instances the poorest were being reached. But institutional, administrative, financial and other constraints mean that many of the poorest are still being missed.

In Bangladesh, for example, the South West Rural Development Project has helped many poor farmers to raise food output, but farmers with holdings of less than an acre are not eligible for membership of the co-operative society through which the project operates and are thus excluded from its benefits. And even though the Grameen Bank project has succeeded in reaching many of the poorest, even here the better motivated and organized poor seem to be more numerous among the borrowers than the very poorest and demoralized poor.

The VDFP in Mali has helped many farmers to double their food output in one of the world's harshest environments. But only villages with recognized associations are eligible for loans — and they tend to be the better-off ones.

Whilst the LISP project in Lesotho has a number of excellent features, there is one aspect of it which acts as a deterrent to the poor being included. People are encouraged to form groups to breed chickens, either in battery or deep-litter style. In practice it is battery units that predominate. Credit is given to allow people to buy a 200-bird battery cage costing around US$350. The people who take out loans (mostly women) have few assets and a commitment to repay a sum of money which is enormous by Lesotho standards — US$350 is more than the average annual income per head. The very poorest are unlikely to be willing to take such a risk. This part of the project is irrelevant to them and inconsistent with IFAD's founding principles. For the very poorest it would be better if the project gave much smaller loans to encourage improved ways of keeping free-range hens; or, alternatively, the deep-litter system would not involve purchasing cages.

IFAD still has some way to go. There may even be an inconsistency between its desire to reach the poorest, risky people as they seem to be, and its role as an international fund. Its 1987 Annual Report, states 'each IFAD project . . . must also satisfy rigorous economic and financial criteria consistent with the norms of international finance'.[10]

And yet are the poorest so risky? The experience of the Grameen Bank suggests not. In a number of other IFAD-funded projects, the poorest have also proved themselves a sound financial risk. But the poor who are disorganized, and find it difficult to satisfy the requirements of official aid projects, have found themselves excluded from fund projects in some countries. This sits uneasily with the agency's claim that no one is beyond reach. No one should be beyond reach, but existing policies make many of them so.

If IFAD has some way to go, for the sake of the poorest, it has to get there. IFAD could help overcome the problems of the disorganized poor by working with NGOs on the spot to help the poorest organize. It has to work with both donor and recipient governments to get over the problem of financial constraints that effectively exclude most of the poor. If the neediest are to be helped then there has to be a positive bias in their favour, and such a bias is likely to make it necessary to put people first, economics second. Somehow this has to

25

be shaped into a coherent framework, a difficult task but vital if the quality of aid is to improve and the poorest are to be reached.

The poorest need to be trusted more, and trusted on the basis of the use they have already made of official aid funds. If official schemes are to embrace the neediest then what seems a risk will often have to be taken. Whilst donors may view this with trepidation, if the very poorest cannot be reached by aid, then its entire rationale might be called into question. Governments, both donor and recipient, need to recognize the dilemma and work with IFAD and other agencies to overcome it for the sake of the poorest.

A more basic question is whether, in any case, official aid policy can go beyond economics and financial rates of return and consider need first, rates of return second. This would entail donor governments relaxing their financial requirements — surely not out of the question as we are talking about *aid* and not a commercial transaction.

IFAD's work has helped some of the poorest; its limited funding has hindered its work but its experience has helped to identify problems. It is therefore making an important contribution. But to claim that its work confirms that 'no people' are too poor to be beyond the reach of effective projects is an overstatement that hides the changes in aid policy which still need to be made. IFAD should ease up on its rhetoric, admit to problems which need to be overcome and build on its valuable work and experience to bring everyone within reach.

## The International Labour Organisation (ILO)

The ILO was established in April 1919 and became, in 1946, the first specialized agency of the United Nations. Its purpose is to contribute to the establishment of peace by promoting social justice and to improve 'through international action, labour conditions and living standards and to promote economic and social stability'.

The vast majority of the world's poorest live in the villages of the developing world, and ILO Convention 141 says that 'the importance of rural workers in the world makes it urgent to associate them with economic and social development action if their conditons of work and life are to be permanently and effectively improved'.

The ILO claims to have become the chief UN agency responsible for encouraging the participation of the rural poor in the development process, and in 1977 it established a programme to this end. The purpose of the programme is to 'promote an equitable and participatory pattern of development through encouragement of autonomous, democratic and self-reliant organizations of the rural poor'.[1]

In April 1985 the ILO drew up guidelines on how participation of the rural poor can be promoted. These were based on field experience: they first looked at the notion of people's participation. This is understood to mean that the poor should have a say in the decisions which affect them, pool their efforts, share risks and responsibilities, as well as resources and benefits, to attain the objectives they themselves set and be allowed to operate within free and independent organizations.

The approach to promoting participation, the guidelines continue, is to help the rural poor develop their own truly independent organizations in accordance with ILO standards and principles. Such organizations may take various forms — trade unions, co-operatives, action committees, associations and movements.

But who is to do the promoting? The task 'requires experts and consultants with a new style of work and experience', say the guidelines. Such initiators need to understand the concepts of participation and be familiar with the successes and problems of participatory projects. What they must not do, however, is act as 'top-down' officials; they need instead to develop their approach with the rural poor themelves:

> Such resource persons can be found in several institutions and from grass-roots experiments in Third World countries, as well as from alternative movements and institutions in industrial countries. They are also emerging from the rural base communities.

The guidelines therefore see non-governmental organization (NGO) workers, including established workers' organizations, playing a central role in promoting participation. Governments and officials who are sympathetic to the concept can advance participation, although big budgets do not necessarily help this kind of work and can even disorient it. Small sums and seed-moneys have been found more appropriate. ILO support for a credit project among refugees in Sudan shows that an official aid agency can get through to the poorest (this project is detailed in Chapter 9). And there have been other successes — in Niger, for instance, where an ILO-supported co-operative development project helped people to establish cereal banks to stabilize prices. The project benefited a highly impoverished group that had previously lacked any outside assistance.

Such projects are, at present, the exception rather than the rule: 'A large majority of beneficiaries of ILO projects are poor', said an ILO official, 'but there appears to be a tendency to target the upper 50 per cent of the poor income groups to the exclusion of the lower 50 per cent.' An ILO-supported refugee project in Somalia, for example, aimed to include the poorest, particularly women heads of households. But it proved difficult to identify the poorest refugees and ensure that they were offered the opportunity to participate. The project staff had to rely on camp authorities and refugee women's leaders to select participants, and this was not always done in a satisfactory way.

A cottage industry project for rural women in Bangladesh provided centres to train rural women in a variety of skills. On completion of the course, the trainees would be helped to obtain access to credit facilities and to market their products. Though the project was designed originally for rural women belonging to the poorest economic strata. It turned out, however, that many trainees were semi-urban women who had a better educational background compared to the national average with only 5 per cent of them being totally illiterate. Their families were generally better off than those of the landless peasants.

At the same time it was observed that the local élites — landowners, tradesmen and moneylenders — were heavily involved in the project. They particpated in the implementation committees which co-ordinated the training centres. An evaluation, carried out in 1988 after the project was completed, observed that, partly because of the active interest of the local élites in the project, most of the trainees came from semi-urban families and did not include an adequate number of the rural disadvantaged who were the target groups of the project.

The ILO has assisted the development of public-works programmes in a number of poor countries. These programmes vary, but usually take the form of a government body undertaking a 'public works' project, employing the

28

poor on its construction and so increasing their incomes, albeit for a short time period. But the poorest do not always get the jobs. A survey of public works projects found that people employed under a project in Burundi, for example, had more education and owned more livestock than the average population. The survey observed that the choice of location for the project was not altogether consistent with the aim of helping the poorest regions and populations.

And the benefits of public-works programmes often go to larger farmers and better-of villages. In an ILO-supported irrigation scheme in Tanzania, the average size of the farms benefiting from the irrigation channels was higher than the average in the project district. Also in Tanzania, a rural water supply project was set up in villages that already had limited supplies not available in other villages. A review of a small-scale irrigation project in Bangladesh observed that in three of the four project areas the average size of the beneficiaries' landholdings was higher than that of the district; on the other hand, the workers employed during the construction phase were clearly from among the poorest. The ILO is doing much valuable work in reaching the poorest but, like IFAD, it still has some way to go.

## The United Nations Development Fund for Women (UNIFEM)

*If you find ways to benefit women . . you help those most in need, for they are at the bottom of the pile in male-dominated Third World societies.*
Good Aid

Talk to people in the huge UN building in New York about UNIFEM and a glazed look will more often than not come over their eyes. Dedicated UN workers will confess they have never even heard of this small organization that is trying to promote women's development.

Under its present name, UNIFEM has only been in existence since 1985; its predecessor, the Voluntary Fund for the United Nations Decade for Women, was set up in 1976. UNIFEM is one of the smallest UN agencies — its annual budget is only around £8m, but smallness allows it a flexibility which is a strength for reaching the poorest peoples.

Whilst accurate statistics are not available, it is highly likely that women account for considerably more than half the 500m people numbered among the world's poorest. The reasons for this are not hard to find. In practically every country, women are to a greater or lesser degree exploited by men. Visiting a village in Mali I talked with a group of women who were drawing water from a well. 'We can't talk much', one of them said, 'we are very tired, our energy is gone, our backs are aching.' Meanwhile the men of the village sat under a nearby tree discussing contemporary affairs, but presumably not the state of women!

In Africa women grow around two-thirds of the food. Often they receive less education and training, are often not allowed to own land and are barely recognized in legal systems. Most policymakers are men. It is men who frame policy for women.

Government policies frequently overlook the needs of women, sometimes showing little or no regard for the contribution that women make. But then housework is not included in national economic statistics, neither is food grown by people for their own consumption. Food policies are too often drawn up with scant regard for helping the women who grow most of the continent's food. Most agricultural extension staff in Africa — the people who advise on how to grow more food — are men, not women. But then most of the students in agricultural colleges are men.

UNIFEM has a dual role. It draws attention to women's needs, supporting national institutions that are working to ensure that women are involved in the mainstream of decisions affecting development rather than be left on the fringe. It also supports practical projects to help low-income women.

The roots of the problem lie deep — more boys than girls are to be found in most schools in the developing world, and it is not surprising that more men than women are in positions of authority. In Gambia, the UNIFEM-supported Gambia Women's Bureau is working for change to allow women to be more involved in the mainstream of development decisions. The bureau started in 1980 in order to advise government on all matters affecting the welfare of women and to promote development activities that would enhance and lift women's status.

Until 1971 not a single woman had ever been employed in the top grade of Gambia's civil service. By 1990, a small but encouraging number of women were employed in the higher reaches of government. More women are undergoing skills-training than in the 1970s: women are being trained as engineers, welders and motor mechanics and there has been an increase in the number of trainee agricultural extension workers. The bureau has also campaigned for, and won, changes in the legal system to help Gambian women, particularly married women. If a wife is deserted, her income is likely to drop, but, until recently, she received little if any compensation. Now she has the legal right to a reasonable sum.

Concerted lobbying by the bureau resulted in changes in the pattern of a rice project in Gambia which was supposed to benefit women but which was failing to do so because women could not own land. A practical project, funded by UNIFEM has supplied milling machines to 15 Gambian villages and saves women hours a day hand-pounding grain, releasing them for other tasks and providing a good example of how to take women into account in a development project (see Chapter 9).

But neither is UNIFEM immune from the problems which beset other agencies which are genuinely trying to get aid to the poorest. Its root-crops project in the Philippines, described in Chapter 7, shows how women who had not attended school are excluded — in practice, the very poorest. The legitimate ambition of project managers to ensure that the project is a success makes it difficult for them to take a chance on people who cannot read or write. Again that is understandable: but again the poorest do not receive any help.

*These three women, who number among the poorest of the poor in Lesotho, are b[...] helped under an IFAD project to grow more food. (Photo: John Madeley)*

*A woman receiving a loan through the Grameen Bank in Bangladesh, an innova[...] credit scheme targeted at the landless labourers. (Photo: IFAD)*

# PART 2: *Some official-aid failures*

## 3 Mali

### Mali Sud: too poor to qualify

IN 1977 THE government of Mali launched the Mali Sud Rural Development Project to try to develop the southern region of this landlocked, Sahelian country. Fertile and underdeveloped, the region has generally good rainfall and vast areas of idle land, the result of shortages of both financial resources and people — under-population being a very real problem. Although Mali is a famine-prone country, the UN Food and Agriculture Organization (FAO) believes that its agricultural potential is one of the best in West Africa, even though little food grows in the arid northern and central regions.

Extended for a further five years in 1983, the Mali Sud project received US$84m for the 1983–8 phase, US$61m of which was foreign aid, US$26m from the World Bank's International Development Association, US$13m from IFAD and the remainder from French and Dutch governments.

The experience of the first eight years contains many lessons for countries which are thinking of embarking on rural development schemes designed to help the poorest. The million and a half people in the project area live in small towns and some 3500 villages. Cotton and a variety of food crops are produced in an area which extends due east from the capital Bamako to the Burkina Faso border, and due south to the Ivory Coast. In the more northerly part of the project area, east of Bamako, annual rainfall of around 400 millimetres (mm) permits only the growth of millet and a limited number of vegetables. Further south, some areas enjoy as much as 1400mm of rain a year.

Responsible for the project is a public body known as the Malian Company for Textile Development (CMDT), a somewhat misleading title for an organization concerned with broadly based rural development. The project's objectives

33

are to: increase the output of maize, sorghum, millet, cotton, cowpeas, rice and livestock; improve financial returns to the farmer; promote village development associations (VDAs), 'securing improvements of agricultural production through applied research'; and raising living standards in the project area through village water supplies and basic health services.[1]

Specific targets included doubling the area of land which grows maize, tripling the output of rice, increasing sorghum and millet production by 50 per cent and raising rural incomes. It was also hoped to increase annual cotton production from 115 000 to 157 000 tonnes. Overall the project was an attempt by the government to overcome famine by regaining the food self-sufficiency the country enjoyed in the 1960s.

In its first eight years, the project's undoubted achievement was that it helped to increase food output. The area under maize increased by around 60 per cent, and output of the staple foods sorghum and millet was stepped up by about 10 per cent, with yields averaging 850kg per hectare in the drought year of 1984, much the same as in years of more normal rains during the early 1980s. Rice output increased with help from Chinese experts, and cotton output also rose.

Some of the project's aims need, however, to be questioned. One aim is to double the output of maize, a crop which demands consistent applications of water. Mali has virtually no irrigation and rainfall is erratic. Although the statistics are impressive — in some regions the area growing maize trebled between 1980 and 1985 and output increased despite drought conditions — there have been disastrous failures.

In Ciesso village, for example, in south-eastern Koutiala region, where people were encouraged to plant maize, the whole of the maize crop was lost in 1984 because of irregular rainfall. Whilst millet and sorghum had been harvested, stores in the village were virtually bare by the end of March 1985, leaving the 2000 villages to face five hungry months before the next harvest. Encouraging some of the world's poorest farmers to grow maize without irrigation is taking a huge gamble with their lives, about which agricultural experts might have been expected to be aware.

## Credit

The Mali Sud project's biggest failing is that it is not helping many of the poorest people in Mali, those who are close to famine. An insufficiently publicized fact of famine in Africa is that only the poorest die. It is they who cannot afford to buy food and, in many cases, are not being helped to grow it.

Under the Mali Sud project, credit and technical advice were offered to farmers who wanted to develop new land and buy seeds, fertilizers and equipment. The project's policy was to give such assistance only through officially recognized VDAs (known locally as *tons*) or villages considered likely to form one. Villages that have received help have clearly bene- fited; standards of living in these villages have generally risen.

But no help was given to villages that do not have a VDA; they are excluded from the project. It is there where a poten- tially good project falls down — whole villages are cut off from a scheme that could be helping them.

VDAs tend to exist in the better-off villages — better off not only in material terms but where there is more motiva- tion and organizational skill. CMDT officials estimated that in 15-20 per cent of villages in the project area, at least 500 of the 3500 villages, there was no chance of a VDA being formed. Yet the people in these villages, which are over- whelmingly the poorest, are the people who need most to be included.

The wealthier villages were able to offer guarantees that they could repay what they borrowed — and some villages are wealthier not just in money terms but also in organiza- tional ability and commitment. The poorer villages were not so lucky, and their experience in 1985 showed the effects of exclusion from the Mali Sud project. The village of Djiguiyara (referred to in the Foreword) is one of the poorest in the area. In March 1985, following two years of drought, its 200 inhabitants were almost destitute. Their harvests had been meagre, food stores were bare, money had run out and people faced starvation.

Engaged in a desperate struggle to stay alive, they were on the brink of being dragged into the African famine. Like others in a similar predicament, they were selling their cattle to raise money for food, even though they rely on cattle for the ploughing season. Yet it was people like them who, above all, needed help from the Mali Sud project, and they were not getting it. In all, over half a million of the country's seven million people left their homes in the spring of 1985 to mi- grate to better-off areas further south.

One of the biggest problems facing Mali's poorest that year was the shortage of seeds for planting. They could not afford seeds and had little chance of obtaining the quite small amounts of credit needed to buy them. With the conditions of the Mali Sud project as they were, people in the poorest, non-VDA villages were unable to borrow and were dependent on voluntary organizations and churches to organize the distribution of seeds to help them. Therefore many of the poorest could not borrow to buy life-saving seeds from a major rural development project run by their own government.

In Mali an official agricultural research station at Cinzana, near the town of Segou, is trying to develop millet seeds that will give higher yields. Probably nothing would help the poorest more than if they could obtain seeds that would enable them to produce twice as much food. But the question is: how are they to get them when they have no money or credit? Unless the poorest are included in projects like Mali Sud then there is a question mark over the value of such research.

Tight credit restrictions are also applied to VDAs which seek a loan from the Mali Sud project. The Zanradougou VDA in the south-east of Mali, near Sikasso, applied for loans to buy cows following an outbreak of disease which killed the cows of 15 out of the village's 19 families. A new cow costs £150, a sum which very few people in the village could afford. The project offered people £120 credit for a cow, leaving them to find the £30 difference. Most were unable to do so; the poorest were again denied credit because they were too poor. Only the richer families were able to buy new cows.

It was unrealistic for the CMDT and World Bank — which as the major aid donor had a large say in the way the project was run — to insist on guarantees from people who have nothing. As it was, this large international aid project was, ludicrously, bypassing people who were close to famine.

Whilst a policy of 'no credit without guarantees' may be safer and understandable in economic terms, it has the distinct disadvantage of leaving out the very poor who most need credit — an omission that may have cost lives in the mid-1980s. A credit programme that meets both need and economic considerations *is* possible. People with a low standard of living are often experts in how to use scarce resources. They have to be to survive. And they are likely to get a high return on the limited amounts they seek to borrow. In countries as diverse as Bangladesh, Sudan and Lesotho the poorest have been loaned money, even though they had no material guarantees to offer, and have proved they could repay.

Official development projects need to prove that they can help those most in need or disillusionment with them will grow — and it will be left to non-governmental organizations to pick up the pieces. If hungry people are offered credit and technical help then an important breakthrough is possible. The key questions confronting policymakers are therefore: Who are the people who are suffering most from under-development? How can projects be geared to helping them? And if there is a risk in lending to the neediest, can aid be mature enough to take it?

When I published an article about the project I was telephoned by an official of the World Bank. He insisted that I had made a mistake and that no villages were excluded from the Mali Sud project. The village of Djiguiyara, he said, must have been outside the project area. This was manifest nonsense as the village was almost in the very centre of the area! But this rather clumsy attempt to gloss over the project's inadequacies appeared to highlight a split between the World Bank and IFAD. The World Bank was keen that credit only be given to those who looked a solid credit risk; IFAD was keener to see that aid reached the poorest. As the stronger partner, the bank got its way but, in this case, IFAD's hand was strengthened by the publicity. Following an article about the project in the May/June 1985 issue of *International Agricultural Development* magazine, this letter was received from Jaap Reijmerink, IFAD project controller:

I refer to your article 'Too Poor to Qualify' about the Mali Sud Rural Development project. You state that the poorest farmers have been excluded from the project. Your worries have been ours since IFAD decided to co-finance the project. As a result the project includes a study on the economic conditions of the present 30 per cent of farmers who are not organized in VDAs; most of them lack agricultural equipment such as a plough, a seeder or oxen. It appears that ownership of such equipment is a critical element in improving yields, production and incomes. I am further pleased to inform you that as a result of discussions between the co-financiers of the Mali Sud project, the CMDT and the BNDA (Banque Nationale pour le Développement Agricole) a draft agreement has been reached under which CMDT will distribute credit to farmers in villages like Djiguiyara [mentioned in the article] where no Village Association has yet been formed, and on terms and conditions which 'take into account the specific economic situation of the farmer'. I hope this information shows that the project is taking into account the conditions of the smaller and poorer farmers and that the modification you seek has already been made [published in the magazine's July/August 1985 issue].

This development was heartening. It exposed the World Bank's attempt to say that the village I visited was outside the area, but, far more important, it shows that organizational problems have no need to stand in the way of the poorest receiving credit. There are ways round the problem — if the will exists to take them. Yet I am still wondering whether such a policy change has been implemented. From seeing a nearby project in Mali 3 years later, also funded by IFAD, it seemed that the lessons had not been applied, and this time there was no World Bank involvement. The following case study shows that, left to its own devices, IFAD was still party to the philosophy of 'no credit except through Village Associations' which again excludes the poorest.


## The Village Development Fund Project (VDFP)

The US$9m VDFP, in the Segou region of Mali, makes low-interest loans to peasant farmers and enjoys a repayment rate that any financial institution would envy — almost 100 per cent. The project, which is almost wholly financed by IFAD, covers an area of the Segou region which is semi-arid, with poor soil, few natural resources, little rainfall, a declining stock of trees but a great deal of sand. Illiteracy among villagers borders on 100 per cent; there are few effective government services. Nearly everyone is poor, although some are poorer than others.

Agriculture is mainly subsistence; the chief crops are millet, sorghum, fonio (a mili/sorghum type grain with good drought-resistance) and, to a lesser extent, cowpeas. Vegetables include potatoes, cabbages, onions and tomatoes.

Groundnuts and peanuts are grown in some villages. Cattle are kept by people who can afford them.

Set up in 1985 the VDFP is clearly benefiting some village communities. The project gives low-interest credit to farmers in 85 of the region's 439 villages, to help them to buy draught oxen, sheep and goats, agricultural tools and fertilizer. Loans are channelled to them through Mali's Banque Nationale pour le Développement Agricole (National Bank for Agricultural Development).

Farmers are charged annual interest of 9 per cent with repayments due over a 5-year period. Those who want a loan put their proposal to a meeting of the village community — and it is an assembly of the whole village that has the final say and which is then responsible for seeing that repayment is made. A community seeking a loan has itself to put down 10 per cent of the value of the money it seeks to borrow.

By 1988 the VDFP had loaned just over US$1m to around 3000 farmers in 85 villages, making the average loan about US$350. Over two-thirds of the money borrowed had been used to buy draught animals which, in turn, helped farmers to extend the area under crops.[2]

Under the VDFP, villages qualify if they are organized into a *ton*, the recognized village unit of organization. But being organized into a *ton* is no guarantee that a village will be included. Villages are selected for inclusion if they satisfy quite tight criteria. VDFP manager, Abdoul Kader Maiga, said that a community must have a record of being trustworthy, it must have social cohesion, with people co-operating well and it must have a good record of paying its taxes (the government imposes a flat-rate tax on all villagers); it must also have the potential to expand the cropping area.[3] 'It is the willingness of people to take advantage of the credit that we are looking for', he said. 'And the project makes it clear that the poorest in the village must gain — if that is not agreed, then there is no loan.' Women farmers have, he said, received loans for gardening activities, also for goats, to try to increase milk supplies.

The project is intended to transform people's mentality', said Abdoul Maiga, 'to encourage them to organise and manage their own affairs. In other words to bring about better trained villagers.'

In a small village called Sinebougou, some 300 miles from Segou, the president of the village committee, Demba Diallo, whose chief crop is millet, was one of the first farmers to receive a loan from the VDFP. He used a US$600 loan to buy three oxen, a plough and several bags of fertilizer. Before receiving the loan he ploughed by hand and could not farm more than five hectares, only about half his land area. Now he says that his oxen enable him to crop double that area and cover ten hectares. In the first two years after taking the loan the fertilizer helped increase the yield of the millet from 600 to 800kg a hectare. His total harvest was over four tonnes a year higher. He kept some of the extra food for his extended family of 20; some he sold in nearby towns.

In total the farmers of Sinebougou village have received 40 oxen from the fund which has enabled them to double the area under crops. Many other villages covered by the project report similar increases. In one of the very poorest areas of Africa more food is therefore being produced for both rural and urban communities.

The project also makes loans available to help people to diversify away from dependence on agriculture and so have more security when drought strikes. Loans have been made for setting up village shops, blacksmithy work, carpentry, trading animals, and for selling salt (which is often difficult to obtain) sugar and petroleum. Villagers have received help to improve literacy skills and health care. Some villagers now have their first-ever literate people.

The innovative nature of the VDFP has brought it into conflict with the Mali Government. It is supposed to have an applied research component, to be carried out under the supervision of existing government institutions. But no research is taking place because of a conflict between the fund and the government institutes. 'The researchers came to us with the ideas which were basically top down', said Abdoul Maiga; 'the project did not want that; we want basic research to be done on farmers' fields and for progress to be built up from there.'

Problems also arose for a seed multiplication centre which again was due to be part of the project. 'An existing seed centre wanted to develop seeds for big farmers, not poorer farmers', said Abdoul Maiga, 'we want to develop drought-resistant seeds which will help safeguard yields when drought strikes.' Mini-seed multiplication centres have now been established in different villages.

The project's interest in improving health-care facilities brought a clash with the Ministry of Health over the best way to go about this. It was agreed eventually that the VDFP should help to train volunteer primary health-care workers. 'The project has made a big impact on health', claimed Abdoul Maiga, 'every village now has its own drugstore.' Repayment rates on loans are good:

> Most credit schemes for small-scale farmers have not worked because they were too flexible [he continued]; extensions to re-payment periods were granted too easily and the farmers got away with too much. We realize when there is a genuine need for an extension of the re-payment period.

The VDFP is working for the villages it covers because they had to satisfy fairly strict criteria before they could be included. Villages that seemed financially shaky and which posed a repayment risk were, however, excluded. The project's careful selection of villages is undoubtedly a key reason for its success; it is also the reason why it has failed to reach people in the very neediest villages.

For villagers covered, the extra area under crops afforded them some shielding from the effects of the severe drought which struck the area in early 1988. In Sinebougou, yields were half the normal but more land was under crops — which meant that the villagers had just about enough food whereas previously they might have experienced severe shortages. But many villagers not covered by the project ended up as famine victims.

The village of Bambougou, for example, was not included in the project. In February 1988 its 800 inhabitants faced starvation after one of the worst harvest in living memory. They were particularly unlucky with the rains, and their food crops were decimated. Whereas the villagers normally harvest around 600kg a hectare of their staple food millet, in October 1987 they harvested only 30kg. 'On most of our fields we had little more than stalks', said a villager, looking over fields that resembled a dustbowl.

The people had little in their barns and very little money to buy food outside the village. 'There are people here who don't know whether they will eat today', said the village headman. But Bambougou did not qualify under the VDFP. The people were badly organized and very poor. In early 1988 many of them sold possessions to raise money for food, or abandoned their homes. A considerable movement of people began — in search of food and work, they trekked

41

hundreds of miles to Mali's more fertile southern regions and also across the border into the Ivory Coast.

Bambougou village lies on the slopes of the River Niger; a simple pump from the river to irrigate the land would give villagers the chance of expanding the area they crop, planting vegetables and enjoying a more nutritious diet. They cannot afford to buy a pump and are not judged credit-worthy enough to borrow money for one. Their need cried out for assistance but they were just too poor for an aid project supposed to help the poor to want to lend them a hand.

Bambougou's experience was not untypical of many of the poorest villages in the region. Not organized well enough to have a *ton* they are excluded from the VDFP. Even if they have a *ton* the criteria for selecting a village for inclusion in the project inevitably mean that villages and peoples who are poorer in social cohesion and community spirit, where they do not work together well for whatever reason, find it difficult to pay their taxes (maybe because of genuine shortages of money), who have limited land and cannot expand their cropping area are not considered eligible for loans.

Such villages are unquestionably 'poorer villages', poor not just in material terms but in many other ways. The people who live there are likely to number among those who do not satisfy the world of official aid projects.

To extend credit to all villages, those without a *ton* and those with a comparatively weak organization, would be to take a risk. Repayment would be more uncertain, the success of the project might be in jeopardy — and what good is a failed project to anyone? Most credit schemes for small farmers have failed in Africa. There was a desire to prove that the VDFP would work — and within its own parameters, work it does. But although poor farmers are receiving help, many of the neediest still look on. The VDFP is still failing *them*.

Abdoul Maiga pointed out that the project is experimental in nature and that there are hopes to extend it with the aid of additional finance — which would certainly be needed if all villages in the region were to be included. But a dangerous gap was opening up in the region between project and non-project villages. The policy of the Mali Government is not helping the project to get aid to the poorest. It appears to be official government policy in Mali that lending is only done to villages who are organized into a *ton*.

Criticisms of the project for failing to reach the poorest are typically met with 'everyone is poor in Mali. The project is reaching some of them.' Within the confines of most credit programmes, including the VDFP, measures can be taken to reach more of the neediest. What the VDFP could do, for example, is to have small teams of people whose sole job it is to help villages without a *ton* to form one. This would be consistent with the project's expressed purpose.

Beyond that lies the wider question of whether IFAD, and the donor countries that fund it, are prepared to get credit through to all villages, even if some appear to present difficulties.

## No market for the nuts

One arm of the VDFP encouraged resource-poor farmers to grow more peanuts, groundnuts and cowpeas. Some farmers who have used loans to buy oxen, agricultural equipment and fertilizer, claimed to have increased their output of such crops as much as five-fold.

When they came to sell these products, there was however a problem — there was no market. A small local demand existed, but no market for the bulk of what they produced.  As they borrowed money to buy supplies to increase output, they had to repay the loans without having income from the nuts. Many could only make those repayments by finding money from elsewhere, sometimes by borrowing from moneylenders or selling possessions.

'The problem is one of over-production', one village president told me. The problem was also that too little thought had gone into examining a vital stage of the food chain. When the project was devised it seemed a good idea to encourage farmers to increase the output of cash crops and so give them a regular cash income — in what had been previously predominantly subsistence villages.

But no one thought hard enough about the market for these extra crops: it was just assumed there would be one. A project document states: 'All incremental production not consumed on the farm would easily be absorbed on the regional or Mali domestic market and/or neighbouring countries.' This proved to be wildly optimistic and completely unfounded.

The project manager, Abdoul Maiga, tried hard to find markets both in Mali and abroad but with little success.

When local traders were approached to buy nuts they offered only a very low price. Again the price offered for cowpeas was so low that it did not cover the costs of production. Attempts were made to sell the surplus in other regions but there is limited purchasing power within Mali. Foreign buyers told Abdoul Maiga that the quantities involved were not large enough for them to buy. There were, for example, 1000 tonnes of surplus cowpeas available. To the small farmers of Segou region, this sounds a hefty amount; foreign buyers said it is not enough. Adding to the villagers' problem is the fact that they had no adequate storage facilities for their surplus foods — something to which the project was begining belatedly to turn its attention.

'Increased output, no market' can spell disaster for poor farmers. The lesson from this part of the project is that markets have to be tested carefully and found *before* small farmers are encouraged to increase their output of market-bound food. It cannot be assumed that firm markets exist; peasant farmers cannot survive on imaginary markets.

Thus the poor farmers of the region who were persuaded to grow nuts ended up not benefiting from the project. For them it was more serious than that — they ended up worse off than they had been before, having to pay for the mistakes of an aid project.

# 4 Missing the poorest in India

A SIZEABLE PROPORTION of the world's poorest people live in India. A national survey in 1983–4 showed that 37 per cent of India's population live below the poverty line — around 275 million people of whom over 220 million live in rural areas.[1] They live in a democracy and under a government that is more committed than many to poverty alleviation, even if that commitment is often honoured more in rhetoric than in substance. But foreign aid to India, substantial as it has been over the years since 1950, seems to have done little to help the poorest out of their poverty.

'The pursuit of growth has been the major plank of anti-poverty policy', says S. Guhan, 'supplemented with fiscal redistribution, better regional balance and encouragement to smaller entrepreneurs in industry, agriculture and the tertiary sectors.'[2] For the poorest, this seems ominous. Aid to help economic growth is, for a start, not likely to trickle down to them. Guhan noted in 1988 that anti-poverty aid has 'firmly entered the agenda of both bilateral and multilateral aid programmes in the last fifteen years or so . . . it has become very much part of the rhetoric of the international community'.[3]

The main plank of the government's anti-poverty strategy has been its Integrated Rural Development Programme (IRDP), which began in 1980. This programme finances, through a combination of loans and subsidies to households below the poverty line, a variety of income-earning schemes to increase the assets of the poorest, including irrigation wells, milch cattle, draught animals, poultry, carts and facilities for small businesses. The IRDP is not supported by foreign aid but is nonetheless worth some mention at as it appears to suffer from many of the same problems of aid-funded projects for the poorest.

In the period of India's Sixth Five Year Development Plan, from 1980 to 1985, the IRDP channelled 17 billion

Indian rupees (Rs) to 17 million families. But on the basis of reports prepared by banks, government agencies and independent field researchers, 'serious drawbacks' were identified, concluded Hansen (in 1987):

A significant proportion of beneficiaries have proved to be households above rather than below the poverty line. These are not eligible for IRDP coverage but have clearly infiltrated the target group because of wilful or faulty identification by the official machinery.[4]

The 'poorest first' principles, laid down in the programme's guidelines, have not operated in practice, and schemes financed under the IRDP have failed to generate incomes to the expected levels. The programme

relies overwhelmingly on government and commercial bank bureaucracies for its delivery system: their motivation, adequacy of training, ability to resist corruption and pressure from a variety of local élites strongly influences the end results.[5]

In short the IRDP suffers from many of the limitations that foreign aid projects for the poorest also meet. The problems of helping the poorest often lie deep in cultural and administrative systems; for a programme to break through, with or without the support of foreign aid, is extremely difficult. Writing in 1987 Hansen said that 'with all its apparent weaknesses, the IRDP is accepted as the current development panacea'.[6]

Such an acceptance of a weak programme as a panacea does nothing for the poorest, although it highlights the fact that the difficulties of getting aid to them are often seen as so enormous that it is easy to give up and settle for second best.

What of aid-funded projects? There are few specific evaluations of their impact on the poorest in India, although there are studies concerning the access of the poor to the benefits of the 'green revolution' and activities such as irrigation, credit, dairying and social forestry that have been popular with aid donors. The benefits of high-yielding seed varieties certainly appear to have gone to more affluent farmers in India, because of the access they have to land, credit, subsidies, extension services and irrigation.

Let us look at just six examples of aid that is either not reaching the poorest, is detrimental to, or a mixed blessing for, them.

## Irrigation

There have been a number of 'big dam' schemes in which the poorest have lost out. India's Madhya Pradesh state, one of the country's poorest, is home to the Bango Dam on the Hasdeo River. Partly funded by the World Bank, this was intended to provide electricity and irrigate 800 000 acres of land, many miles away. But some 70 000 acres are being flooded, 29 villages submerged and 3000 families flooded out of their homes. Few received compensation.

An official of the aid agency Oxfam described one village he visited:

> The whole village had just received duplicated letters stating that they had been allocated 150 square feet for their houses at the new site. They had no idea what this meant and were shocked when we showed them a room of that size. Charan Sai's house measures around 400 square feet, with a further 800 square feet for bullocks and household jobs. His newly acquired plot will have to do everything that the existing 1200 square feet does — on just one eighth of the size.[7]

The US$100 million Bhima Command Area Development Project has helped farmers in the arid region of the Deccan Plateau in Maharshtra, some 350km south-east of Bombay, to increase food output, alleviate their poverty and improve the nutrition of themselves and their families. The project has made irrigation available to change the traditional rain-fed agriculture of the area, which is subject to frequent drought, to an irrigated, multiple-cropping area capable of improving yields.

Partly funded by IFAD the project began in 1980 and was developed in the context of India's development planning as one of six schemes designed to speed up the rate of new irrigation in Maharashtra. It has brought year-round irrigation water within reach of nearly 100 000 people who live in farming villages in the area's 189 villages. Small farmers, those owning five hectares or less, make up over 60 per cent of these families.

The irrigation system operates through a recently completed dam, the Ujjani, a reservoir and a network of canals. Through the system, water is provided to each farm at a flow of 30 litres per second, which is roughly the amount that the farmers needs for his crops. A rotational water-supply system

47

has been introduced whereby a fixed period of time is allotted to each farmer receiving water; this ensures equitable distribution.

Farmers were initially reluctant to take advantage of the irrigation and there were also construction problems. By 1988 the percentage of the area for which year-round and full benefits are available was still small — 6716 hectares or about 11.6 per cent of the planned area. Because of the problems with the canal construction works, some of the farmers can only receive irrigation water during the autumn and winter.

Both yields and incomes have increased, in some cases substantially. Yields on those farms which are benefiting from year-round irrigation have risen from about 0.4 tonnes per hectare (t/ha) to an average 1.28t/ha for jowar (sorghum), and from 0.70 to 1.45t/ha for groundnuts. Sugar-cane yields have increased from 85 to 140t/ha. Farmers with only autumn and winter irrigation have also increased their yields in a more limited way. While, however, the irrigation has led many farmers to seize the opportunity to get more from their land, there have been wide variations. Yields of wheat have varied from between 5 to 40 quintals a hectare and of jowar from between 6 to 30 quintals. This suggests that agricultural supplies were not available when they were needed.

The average net income earned by the year-round beneficiaries was Rs4640 per ha in 1985-6 as compared to Rs1277 for farmers with only winter season irrigation and Rs455 in non-irrigation areas. IFAD claims that the reduction of poverty in the areas receiving year-round water is considerable — that before commencement of the project, only 39 per cent of the farm households were living above the official poverty line but that by 1986 the number of beneficiary households living above this level had nearly doubled, to 74 per cent.

A spin-off from the project has been the stimulus it has given to development in the area. Increased groundnut production, for example, has given an impetus to investment in oil-crushing units: new units were initially being set up at the rate of over 50 a year and each employed about five people. The additional activity in groundnut crushing has led to increased production of oilcake which serves as a valuable cattle feed. The increased flow of rural development has helped to slow down the flow of people migrating from the area. Before the project started, many small and marginal farmers were leaving their villages in search of employment. With the introduction of irrigation, people no longer have to migrate to find work and have returned to their villages to lead a settled life.

The Bhima project therefore has many favourable aspects. But it has a negative side. An IFAD evaluation reports had this to say:

> Some people have also been hurt by the project. The Bhima Reservoir inundated 29,000 hectares and some 57,000 people had to be relocated due to the submergence. The relocation programme has been a very bitter experience for some people. It is a sad commentary that . . . four years after completion, thirteen more villages where people are to be resettled are still not ready for occupation.[8]

What also seems to have happened is that many women in the project area were burdened with increased livestock responsibilities. With the additional earnings the predominantly male farmers purchased more draught and milch animals. It was the women who were expected to look after them, usually for nothing, which merely increased the amount of unpaid work they do.

Too little thought had therefore gone into helping the people due to be resettled (the people who lived in the villages due to be submerged), and to the effects on the poorest, the women. A more sensitive and thoughtful approach to matters such as these when the project was being designed and planned could have offset the suffering of the poorest.

## Health

The Norwegian Government is aiding the All India Hospitals Post Partum Programme which provides family-planning services, maternity and child-care schemes, and health and nutrition education. In practice it has 'primarily been a programme for the delivery of female sterilizations', according to Stein Hansen, 'with additional services provided for antenatal and maternity care, including abortions.'[9]

But an important limitation of the programme, Hansen points out, was that even after it had been extended to sub-district level, it still did 'not reach the majority of poor rural women, who have little or no access to services, unless there is a conscious attempt to reach women'. Poorer women are handicapped, said Hansen,

> by their poor status in the family and society, the remoteness of their villages from district and sub-district centres and their lack of knowledge about the programmes. Thus without an effective community-based infrastructure and maternal and child health delivery, the provisions of ante- and post-natal care and under-five immunisation are severely limited.

One needs to question, according to Hansen, whether this programme was

> appropriate for support by a donor who is aiming at poverty alleviation . . . it would be more logical to assist directly programmes for maternal and child health care, literacy and education for women. Such programmes could ensure that women make their own conscious choices regarding reproductive control and gain confidence.

Integrated Child Development Services (ICDS), a major Government of India programme launched in 1975 during the Fifth Five Year Plan, is a social development programme receiving Norwegian aid. The programme operates in a limited number of rural blocks and poor urban settlements in all states.[10] It was the first attempt at an integrated approach to the physical, social and psychological development of the child. The objective is to develop a delivery model for welfare services for the age group 0 to 6 years, and for pregnant and lactating mothers. The cornerstone of the model is the *anganwadi* (or health and education centre) at village/poor urban settlement level. It is operated by a grass-root level worker — the *anganwadi* worker.

The services provided by the *anganwadi* are:

○ health check-ups of children in the age group 0 to 6 years, and pregnant mothers;
○ supplementary nutrition for children in the age group 0 to 6 years, and for lactating and pregnant mothers;
○ immunization of all children in the age group 0 to 6 years, and of pregnant women;
○ treatment of minor ailments and the referral of children in the age group 0 to 6 years, and of pregnant mothers;

o nutrition and health education for women; and
o non-formal, pre-school education for the age group 3 to 6 years.

In operation, the programme has had a number of problems. Its success hinges on the motivation and capability of the *anganwadi*. They are, for the most part, women with little education who are underpaid and overworked. They receive very little practical help from the supervisory structure which sometimes operates as a policing system rather than an enabling one.

The operation of the centres is handicapped by lack of infrastructure. In most places there are no separate buildings to house the *anganwadi* activities, and it is very difficult to hold pre-school activities without buildings. In other cases the pre-school activities often deteriorate into highly regimented, poorly run formal classroom situations.

The nutrition programme suffers in many areas because of poor management. The health aspects of the programmes are dependent on the co-ordination between the government health infrastructure (which in most parts of India is weak at the local levels) and the ICDS programme. The activities for women are often not treated as an integral part of the programme.

Despite these deficiencies, Hansen considered the programme as one of the most successful in reaching the poorest and most vulnerable sections of society:

o it has a good chance of having a sustained nutritional impact on poor children in the most vulnerable period of their lives (0 to 6 years);
o it relieves the domestic work-load of working-class mothers in rural and poor urban settlements;
o it creates an opportunity for engaging women in education and subsidiary income occupations;
o it provides the best available opportunity of delivering health care to the most vulnerable sections of the population, namely mothers and children;
o it is a programme which employs primarily women; and it is therefore an opportunity for women workers to develop skills and become key workers in development.

But the problem with labelling projects like this a 'success' is that the shortcomings can be masked and nothing done about them.

## Credit

Credit can be a vital way of reaching the poorest but credit which is used to buy tractors is virtually guaranteed to make the poor poorer, according to Paul Mosley, writing in 1987.[11] Yet aid from the World Bank and the British government's Overseas Development Administration (ODA) has allowed farmers in India, in practice the richer farmers, to secure credit to buy tractors and combine harvesters. Inevitably this has been to the detriment of the poorest.

> In some areas of northern India [said Mosley], such as Punjab and Haryana, the extra demands for labour imposed by the green revolution have caused increases in wages, and larger farmers have been tempted to counteract these increases by purchase of machinery. These purchases have since the early 1970s been financed through India's National Bank for Agricultural and Rural Development (NABARD) which is in turn supported by the World Bank and ODA through long-term aid programmes.[12]

According to Mosley, neither the World Bank or the ODA:

> has shown proper awareness of the need to press NABARD not to use its lending for this purpose if the poverty-reduction aims of the current Indian five-year plan are to be realized. The lesson of not giving aid directly in tractor form has now, it seems, been learnt; but not the dangers inherent in credit programmes which can be diverted to secure the interests of rich farmers.[13]

## Fertilizer

Launched in 1982, the British government aid-funded Indo-British Fertilizer Education project (IBFEP) is claimed to be one of the largest 'poverty-focused' agricultural extension schemes in South Asia.[14] Britain has given aid of £30 million to the project which, it is claimed, affects 125 000 farmers and 4500 villages.

The official view, say Steve Percy and Mike Hall, is that IBFEP is 'the most successful, best focused and most effective of British aid projects in India'. The project has encouraged people in the states of Assam, Bihar, Madhya Pradesh, Orissa, Uttar Pradesh and West Bengal to use more fertilizer and higher-yielding seed varieties (HYVs).[15]

'The scheme works on the model farm principle', according to Percy and Hall. Each year two villages and an area of approximately 62 hectares are taken. As Indian agronomist, Mimai Pal, told them:

> The majority of farmers are small and marginal, owning less than two hectares; they are supplied with HYVs, fertilisers and pesticides at a 50 to 30 per cent subsidy. Technical advice is given throughout.

Yields in the demonstration areas have increased by 79 per cent, according to the Hindustan Fertiliser Corporation, say Percy and Hall. But as a British aid official told them, this was hardly surprising in view of the assured supply of inputs. 'What is in doubt is the value of the project for poorest farmers', they say. They cite one farmer, Sabash, who owns less than one eighth of a hectare of unirrigated land which yields one crop a year: 'His soil is poor . . . he owns no bullocks . . . the state bank is closed to him.' Sabash quickly abandoned the new technology after the demonstration period. 'When fertilisers and pesticides are in short supply he has neither the money nor the influence to acquire them. And often the risk is too great; with little capital he is on a loser if the seeds are poor quality.'

Some small farmers with rather more land than Sabash are doing well from the scheme but this only illustrates that this is a project for the 'not so very poor'. The very poorest cannot take the risks that the 'not so very poor' can take, and so the project only widens rural inequalities, leaving the neediest behind.

These examples, drawn from many, pose a number of questions:

○ Does official aid try to involve the neediest?
○ Does it ask them what they want?
○ Does it ask, for example, whether there is an effective community-based health infrastructure in place before 'health' aid is given? Knowing the likelihood that aid will not reach the poorest unless such infrastructure is in place, do donors help to put it in place before doing anything else?
○ Why do donors continue to support large dam schemes which displace poor people? And if they must back such schemes, why do they do nothing to ensure a proper deal for those people?

In overall terms, India is the world's largest recipient of aid — it received US$4.5 billion in 1989 — but in terms of aid per head it is also one of the smallest.

Aid has supported growth and it has helped to avert crises, but there has been an increase in the number of absolute poor and, in its present form, most aid is not helping the poorest. Guhan concludes that

> very little can be said on the impact of aid on poverty . . . except that, but for aid, poverty might have got worse. . . It seems that not much of the (limited) aid available for the poverty-orientation portfolio has proved to be particularly poor-specific.[16]

The snag is that whilst the government makes the right noises about poverty alleviation, it tends to rule out any major structural changes. Land reform, for example, is not promoted vigorously, and is implemented even less vigorously. There has been little encouragement of redistribution of assets to the poorest.

One of the consequences, and perhaps the cause, of poverty and its associated ills 'has been the generally low level of organization of the poor', says Hansen.[17] Apart from places such as Kerala, the poor have remained largely unorganized whilst richer peasants were forming their own organization. 'An absence of a powerful organisation', points out Hansen, 'has deprived the rural poor from even those ameliorative measures that legislation and public policy provide for them.'

It is clear that both national and international aid are failing to reach most of India's poorest people. Whilst structural changes are needed in India if the poor are to benefit from development, a higher volume of foreign aid, if properly directed in small amounts to community-based schemes where there is substantial local participation, could make a significant contribution to improved livelihoods.

# 5 British aid to Bangladesh[†]

## MARK ROBINSON

*The urgency has gone from attempts to directly help the poorest.*

ActionAid report, 1987.

## The dimensions of rural poverty

POVERTY IS A condition which affects the vast majority of Bangladeshis, especially in rural areas. Although the conditions of slum-dwellers and the destitute in Dhaka and other cities can be very bit as harsh and miserable as those of the landless in the countryside, in terms of sheer numbers, it is rural Bangladesh which contains the large majority of people who live in situations of absolute poverty. This is why measures are needed to assess the extent of poverty. There can be a world of difference between poverty in the form of low standards of living and poverty defined as living on the brink of starvation.

One widely used poverty line in Bangladesh is based on estimates made by the World Health Organization of the bare minimum of calorific consumption necessary to meet human energy requirements. On this basis over two-thirds of the population are subsisting below the poverty line.

The significance of this becomes brutally apparent given that consumption levels below 90 per cent of the minimum calorific intake are considered inadequate for people to lead an active working life, while consumption levels of 80 per cent and below are known to result in stunted growth and serious risk to health. In Bangladesh, a second poverty line

---

† Adapted with permission, from *Aid for the Poorest? UK Aid to Bangladesh*, ActionAid/ODI, London, 1988. The author is a Research Fellow at the Overseas Development Institute, London.

(85 per cent of minimum calorific intake) is used to distinguish those in absolute poverty. More than half the rural population and one third of the urban population are currently below this figure.

Land is the prime source of wealth in rural Bangladesh, and the size of landholding also provides an indicator of poverty. Two-and-a-half acres is considered the minimum to sustain a peasant household in Bangladesh, and yet 70 per cent of farms are below this size. As a result, most farmers are forced to seek work on the fields of richer landowners, or hire in additional land on a sharecropping basis. Rural areas also contain a large number of people who are engaged in non-farm employment, for example rickshaw pullers, and a large proportion of these are also below the poverty level. The very poorest groups in rural society are those owning neither land nor any other assets of their own; they have to rely almost entirely on external sources of income, principally working as farm labourers on a day-to-day basis.

Some evidence has shown that average rural incomes were, slowly rising in the early 1980s. But work is rarely available on a year-round basis, and most labourers are employed for only six months of the year. Employment on food-for-work programmes provides relief for a small proportion of the landless labour force during the slack season but contributes little to their capacity for longer-term self-sufficiency.

Women from landless households, who are generally inhibited from working in fields through purdah restrictions, often husk rice and perform domestic tasks for wealthier households. In the last resort, they are forced to abandon such restrictions and turn to especially onerous labour such as stone-breaking or working on construction projects, where they work long hours in return for very low wages.

One major factor stands out when considering the extent of rural poverty in Bangladesh. Poverty is not caused purely by pressure on resources brought about by a growing population; it stems from and is perpetuated by an unequal access to resources which in turn limits the capacity of poor people to improve their livelihoods.

There is a wide measure of agreement, among donors particularly, over which policy measures would require implementation to achieve a genuine shift of power and resources in favour of the poor. Three major ones stand out:

○ the introduction of measures designed to enforce and extend present legislation on land reform;
○ a sustained increase in the production of foodgrains through measures aimed at enhancing productivity of land and labour;
○ the creation of non-farm employment through the establishment of agro-industry, an extension of rural services and the provision of resources for income-generating activities.

Given the political sensitivity of land reform, it is highly unlikely that the government will take steps to ensure a more equitable distribution of land, even if donor pressure were forthcoming. The allocation of small parcels of unused government land to the rural poor is piecemeal in nature and will affect only a small percentage of the landless population; it does not address the existing pattern of land distribution in the countryside which continues to favour the rural rich at the expense of small farmers and the landless.

In the absence of any concerted effort on the part of the government to implement effective land redistribution, the emphasis of development assistance programmes is on the promotion of higher agricultural growth, land reclamation and, to some extent, non-farm employment. It is unquestionable that increased foodgrain output is a desirable objective; but greater output does not automatically entail a reduction in hunger. If the aim is to improve both the quantity and quality of food consumed by the rural poor, then raising the incomes of those poor to purchase food must also feature prominently in development strategies. Vulnerable-group feeding schemes and food-for-work programmes help prevent starvation; but self-sufficiency for the rural poor means having the resources for purchasing food, clothing and shelter. This is the crux of poverty-focused development.

Under such conditions, foreign aid is widely held to be crucial in helping to alleviate poverty by financing a large proportion of the development budget of the Bangladesh government.

International aid began to pour into Bangladesh in response to the catastropic cyclone of 1971 which caused in the region of half a million deaths. Initially, aid was predominantly in the form of disaster relief and food shipments.

Three years later, as the economy was beginning to recover from the effects of the war which led to independence, the disastrous floods of 1974 set back the process of reconstruction. It was evident that the country would require large quantities of foreign aid for many years to come. Over the course of a fifteen-year period between 1971 and 1986 some US$20 billion of official aid has been committed to Bangladesh, only three-quarters of which were actually disbursed.

Some countries, notably Japan, the USA and the Federal Republic of Germany, have provided a large proportion of their aid in the form of concessional loans. Others, such as the UK and members of the Like-Minded Group (Canada, Sweden, Norway, Denmark and the Netherlands) have provided almost all of their aid as grants. Aid commitments in 1988 were in excess of US$1.5 billion per year. The largest single aid donor to Bangladesh is the World Bank, followed by the Asian Development Bank.

## The role of British aid

Britain has been providing aid to Bangladesh since its establishment as a separate independent state in 1971. Current bilateral aid spending in excess of £50 million a year makes Bangladesh the second largest recipient of development assistance from the UK. Additional assistance is provided from multilateral organizations to which Britain contributes, including the European Community, which has a large food programme. The priority given to Bangladesh in Britain's aid programme is justified on the grounds that it is one of the poorest countries of the world.

British bilateral aid is provided in accordance with the objectives set out in the Third Five Year Plan of the Government of Bangladesh. In the words of an Overseas Development Administration (ODA) publication:

> Britain's aid policy is to help Bangladesh meet its development objectives, and to ensure that the benefits of development reach the poorest . . . the ODA specializes in assistance to those sectors where British goods and services can be provided at a comparative advantage to those of other donors.

The energy sector is the largest recipient of project aid from the UK, and ODA currently regards power-generation as an essential precondition for industrial development. The

Greater Dhaka Power Project has been assisted by Britain since 1974 and by 1988 over £30 million worth of British aid had been provided. The project aims to extend the electricity supply system in Dhaka to cater for industrial requirements and domestic demand. There has been criticism that new transmission lines have principally benefited better-off residential areas and that there is an excessive focus on the needs of the capital at the exclusion of rural areas. For its part, ODA claims that there has been considerable job creation as a direct result of industrial development, which receives a stimulus from the increased availability of electricity.

A further extension of the project, designed to improve transmission and power distribution, is budgeted at some £50 million, which means that it is likely to absorb a major share of the project-aid allocation for some time to come. In transport infrastructure, ODA has provided £12 million for bridge construction and design. In addition, a part of the £25 million British commodity-aid allocation in 1987 to 1988 was used to procure construction materials for bridges and for pontoons.

ODA's case for concentrating aid on capital projects is based on the overall and long-term economic development needs of the country. In the shorter run, some employment will inevitably have been generated but critics point out that the direct benefits to the rural poor are limited and they claim that the main immediate beneficiaries are British companies. ODA itself has recognized that development projects in the rural sector have a greater potential for directly improving the lives of the poor majority and point to what they regard as a substantial record of support for the renewable natural-resources sector and for family planning and health provision.

ODA currently funds five projects in the agricultural sector. Three of these are major projects accounting for a large share of the resources allocated to the sector by ODA. Two, the Second Rural Development Project and the Second Deep Tubewells Project, are World Bank-led initiatives in which ODA funds discrete project components. The third project is the Tea Rehabilitation Project, which the ODA has supported since 1979 in collaboration with the European Community.

A further major project being implemented by ODA in rural Bangladesh is in the social and community service sector. This is the Third Family Health and Population Project, again on a co-financing basis in association with the World Bank and a number of other donors.

## The Second Rural Development Project (RDII)

RDII was launched by the Government of Bangladesh in 1983. The aim of the project is to increase agricultural production and rural employment by strengthening rural co-operatives. The intention is also to transform co-operatives into commercially viable enterprises in order to ease the pressure on government resources.

RDII was designed to replicate what has been termed the 'Comilla model' of integrated rural development throughout the country. This approach, developed by the Academy for Rural Development over the course of the 1960s, centred on the creation of multipurpose co-operatives composed of small and economically marginal farmers, with the objective of improving methods of cultivation and foodgrains production.

At the village level, primary societies aimed to provide credit, mobilize savings, distribute agricultural inputs and co-ordinate the marketing of produce. These were then federated at the *upazilla* level (local administrative areas below the district level, previously called *thanas*) where the central co-operative association provided more sophisticated services such as storage, marketing of inputs, maintenance of irrigation machinery, and the processing of produce. The associations also performed an important administrative function in raising and approving loans for the primary societies.

The basic model was extended to other parts of the country under the aegis of what became the Integrated Rural Development Programme. This was subsequently renamed the Bangladesh Rural Development Board (BRDB) which became the government agency responsible for the implementation of RDII.

One of the principal components of the project has been the provision of credit to co-operative members for the purchase of minor irrigation equipment and tool kits. This has been supplemented with improved irrigation and crop marketing, and short-term credit for crop production. In line with the objective of strengthening the co-operative structure, there has been an emphasis on the construction of new office facilities and staff training.

The World Bank is providing the major source of finance with a concessional loan of US$100 million. Among other bilateral donors, the Canadian International Development Agency (CIDA) is funding a component called the Rural Poor Programme with a grant of US$17 million. This has the aim of making credit available to the landless through specially established co-operatives.

ODA support is centred on the training of co-operative managers and the strengthening of the audit capacity of co-operatives at a total cost of US$11 million (£7 million). The bulk of this is in the form of capital aid for the local-cost component for civil works, staff salaries and operating expenses, and for the purchase of vehicles and training equipment from Britain.

Recognizing that under previous programmes many co-operatives were in effect controlled by a small number of richer farmers, ODA placed a major emphasis on the managerial role of BRDB, and on strong supervision by the central co-operative societies at the *upazilla* level in order to curb local nepotism. Better auditing procedures were judged to be important for detecting corruption, the mismanagement of co-operative accounts and inefficiency. ODA justified its involvement in training and improved co-operative management on the grounds that institutional development was central to the project's success and to ensure that the poorer farmers had the opportunity to gain a fair share of the benefits.

The project as a whole did not finally get off the ground until 1985, two years behind schedule, and progress to date has been unsatisfactory. An FAO mid-term evaluation conducted in 1987 concluded that RDII had not succeeded in its objective of promoting the co-operative structure on an autonomous basis and a more recent World Bank progress report observed that the co-operative system was 'far from reaching the project goal'. There has been no attempt thus far to evaluate the impact of the project on agricultural production, but expectations of a potential 7 per cent increase in overall food production appear to have been optimistic.

A number of problem areas have already been identified:

○ co-operatives have been unable to provide members with services other than credit;

61

○ credit recovery rates remain low, at around the 60 per cent mark;
○ a high incidence of misappropriation by co-operative officers has affected one out of six central co-operative societies.

The two components of the project that have been relatively successful in achieving their objectives are the Rural Poor Programme (RPP) and the training and auditing inputs from ODA. Despite having rather poor loan-recovery rates, the RPP has succeeded in setting up more landless co-operatives than originally envisaged. By extending credit through these co-operatives, the programme is seen as having made some progress in providing the landless, and women in particular, with job opportunities and the means to generate incomes. ActionAid, in a different approach, has also attempted to establish credit programmes which are 'burglar proofed' from seizure by the better-off.

The training courses designed by ODA for BRDB officials and co-operative managers have, by and large, been regarded in a favourable light and a further stage of the project aims to provide training for co-operative members at the village level. However, on the auditing side, while a backlog of some 60,000 co-operative accounts has been cleared, the quality of the accounts themselves have not improved significantly.

A number of different reasons have been put forward to explain the shortcomings of the project. The World Bank and the other donors tend to stress administrative deficiencies on the part of BRDB and the central co-operative associations. In order to redress these, they have recommended changes in the arrangements governing credit provision and loan recovery, including, for example, the taking of punitive action against defaulting co-operatives. Yet such actions fail to address some of the more fundamental problems related to the use of the co-operative structure as a mechanism to promote rural development. A principal problem concerns the social composition of the co-operatives themselves.

Many of the village primary societies, far from representing the interests of a large number of small and marginal farmers, are in effect controlled by a handful of wealthier individuals drawn from the powerful families in the village. As a result, the bulk of the benefits accruing from credit provision is monopolized by such families. Co-operatives are clearly susceptible to domination by influential landholding groups and this has meant that the rural poor have not been, in very many cases, the principal beneficiaries of the project as a whole.

For ODA, this means that while auditing of the co-operative accounts may help to identify defaulters and curb misappropriation, and while training can improve accountability and inspire motivation among co-operative officials, the success of such initiatives will be curtailed by the structures into which they are inserted. Taking training down to the primary societies at the village level will no doubt help to involve more members in decision-making but it is unlikely to solve the basic underlying problem of social composition. While ODA's project components can be considered successful in themselves, poor performance of the overall project is likely to blunt their intended impact.

## The Second Deep Tubewells Project

In line with the Bangladesh Government's objective of increasing food production, the Second Deep Tubewells Project is primarily designed to expand irrigation capacity in the dry season. The original aim of the project was to install 4000 deep tubewells (DTWs) with an irrigation potential of 320 000 acres. These DTWs are sold to farmers' co-operatives under the auspices of a government agency, the Bangladesh Agricultural Development Corporation (BADC). In this way, the project was deliberately intended to act as a stimulus to the co-operative movement, thereby providing a linkage with RDII. Initially, the project area covered 37 *upazillas* in the centre of the country, though this was later extended to 60 *upazillas*.

The World Bank is the principal donor, providing concessional loans to the government for use as credit for the purchase of tubewells by the co-operatives. ODA is spending up to £17 million, a large proportion of which is used for the purchase of diesel engines and ancillary equipment. It also supports a technical co-operation input from the project consultants, who provide advice on tubewell management, run training courses for operators and monitor the progress of tubewell installations.

DTWs are designed to tap groundwater reserves which are typically several hundred feet under the surface. The tubewells mostly run on diesel, though some are electrically operated, and they require skilled operators and continuous maintenance. This means that they are expensive to purchase and costly to manage, placing them well beyond the reach of individual smallholders. It is for this reason that a decision was made to make DTWs available to co-operatives in order to spread the costs between farmers.

Applications for DTWs submitted to BADC by farmers' co-operatives for approval are only considered if the application is made by a properly formed co-operative with an acceptable credit rating and good loan-repayment record. Once the co-operative has been declared eligible for a loan, drilling and installation can then take place, provided a favourable site survey has been undertaken.

The project has been fraught with difficulties from its start-up, effectively in 1984 to 1985 when drilling began in earnest. There is a strong emphasis in the project on maximizing the amount of land that can be irrigated by an individual tubewell. An Irrigation Management Programme aims to develop this 'command area' potential through improvements in feeder channels and distribution systems. In practice, average command areas have been well below the 80 acres target set at the beginning of the project, and it has taken a major 'task-force' initiative (with ODA support) to improve the command area of under-performing wells. This has brought the average command area up to 55 acres, which is higher than most other DTW schemes in Bangladesh. Delays in delivery and the poor performance of individual tubewells have had an adverse impact on demand.

Farmers are reluctant to make substantial investments if they have to wait months before the tubewell is actually installed and operating. Under-performance combined with operating difficulties have also led to inadequate returns on investment for many co-operative farmers, and this in turn has created problems in meeting repayments and in financing running costs.

Since the project is primarily concerned with increasing the irrigation area in order to raise foodgrain production, attention has focused almost exclusively on targets relating to tubewell installation and performance. But the project has been criticized on the grounds of equity, namely that inadequate attention was paid to the social implications of DTW development.

Many of the 'poverty focus' problems associated with RDII may have also beset the Deep Tubewells Project, as tubewells are sold to co-operatives. There are instances where richer farmers have exerted influence over siting of tubewells and over payment contributions. Against this, evaluation studies undertaken by the project consultants on selected sites have demonstrated that the benefits accruing from tubewell installation have been shared in proportion to landholding between individual co-operative members. Only a more extensive evaluation would reveal whether this is the case for most of the sites, or if the benefits have been monopolized by a handful of wealthier farmers in a significant number of co-operatives, as critics of the project allege (see, for example, M. Howes, *Whose water?*, 1985. Inasmuch as the project is aimed at co-operative farmers, it does not benefit the landless, except in terms of some increase in employment opportunities.

## How small farmers lose out

Other 'poverty-focussed' projects in Bangledesh fall into the same trap as the British aid programme. The $30 million IFAD-funded South-west Rural Development Project is an example. The project aims to help low-income farmers to make the switch from rainfed to irrigated agriculture and thereby to increase their output of foodgrain.

Located in Jessore and Faridpur districts, which are among the poorest in the country, the project makes credit available to small farmers. Priority is given to those with holdings of less than three acres of land (such farmers work about a third of the holdings in the project area). Farmers only qualify however if they are members of Farmers' Co-operative Societies. The credit has helped beneficiaries to buy irrigation equipment, HYVs, fertilizer and insecticide for the newly irrigated crops.

By the end of 1987, after the project had been running for five years, 350 DTWs and 3585 shallow tubewells had been installed, and farmers were reaping the benefits. Rice production and earnings had increased, and sometimes had more than doubled. The increases in rice output made a major contribution to food security by reducing dependency on the monsoon crop, which is destroyed by floods one year in three.

The project has encouraged the landless to participate in the co-operative system, by establishing landless co-operatives as well as enrolling landless sharecroppers in farmers' co-operatives. Landless labourers have benefited from higher incomes as a result of increased employment during the dry season.

But there is, however, a problem. The very small and usually the very poorest farmers, those with holdings of less than an acre, are not eligible for membership of the co-operative society. They are therefore excluded from access to the irrigation development under the project. These very small farmers make up about a third of the farmers who farm less than three acres. Often they rent land as sharecroppers; usually they have no means of their own to buy inputs and their incomes are low, often too low for survival. Nor has the extension of irrigation improved income distribution among smallholders; benefits to be derived from irrigation equipment depend on the size of farms.

A project designed to help the poor has therefore run into an institutional problem, in this case the rules of co-operative societies. Again this raises the importance of donors spotting difficulties like this beforehand and suggesting, or insisting on changes.

An IFAD evaluation document on the project says the irrigation 'increases the farmers' interest in investing in high-yielding variety seeds and fertilisers'. It is not difficult to see how such investment can widen the gap between farmers with over an acre of land, who qualify under the project, and those with less, who are excluded.

## Conclusions

As the British bilateral aid programme in Bangladesh is concentrated on energy and communications infrastructure it can have a significant long-term impact on the Bangladesh economy and indirectly, therefore, have a potential impact on the poor's living standards and employment prospects. But, in the short to medium term, it is the interests of industry and urban areas which benefit most.

The bulk of the poor are in rural areas and British project aid to the agricultural sector is currently only 17 per cent of the total volume of its bilateral aid. It would be desirable to increase the proportion of British aid going directly to agriculture and rural development in Bangladesh as it is only through raising the incomes of the rural poor that a significant impact on alleviating poverty will be achieved.

Support for projects in the agricultural sector is not of course synonymous with poverty alleviation. Very little of ODA project aid can be considered poverty-focused in the strict sense of identifying the needs of the poorest as the primary consideration. The only existing projects which are designed specifically with the intention of benefiting the poorest groups are those supported in collaboration with non-governmental organizations through the Joint Funding Scheme. There are however individual project components which are targetted at the poor.

In projects designed to improve conditions for the rural population, it has proved difficult to prevent opportunities and benefits from being monopolized by wealthier social groups. The general record of both RDII and the DTWs project is that the provision of credit and tubewell installation has tended to be of most advantage to better-off members of co-operatives.

There are clearly considerable limits on the capacity of donors to prevent such a capturing of benefits, although it can be argued that the projects were insufficiently grounded in poverty considerations — either the needs of the very poor were not taken into account or obstacles preventing benefits from reaching the poor were not properly anticipated. Both stem from a failure to investigate the complexities of the social structure in rural Bangladesh. Considerations such as the distribution of credit between different categories of farmers are difficult to measure, but a truly poverty-focused approach needs to address such problems.

In practice, of course, official bilateral aid must recognize the development priorities set by the Government of Bangladesh which in turn places constraints on the ability of donors to explore alternative avenues for channelling aid in a poverty-focused direction. But the example set by members of the Like-Minded Group suggests that donors do have some influence in negotiating with the government over poverty-alleviation issues, enabling them to adopt approaches which place the needs of the poor at the forefront of project design.

# 6 Lending to the poorest: early lessons from the Small Farmers' Development Programme (SFDP), Nepal[†]

## PAUL MOSLEY and RUDRA PRASAD DAHAL

LACK OF ACCESS to credit can be a serious obstacle to agricultural growth in regions where farmers have very small landholdings and/or lack of secure title to the land they work. Conventional banks are reluctant to lend without collateral, and any small loans they make will, by virtue of their smallness, be expensive to appraise, to administer and to supervise. One of the most ambitious experiments in lending to small farmers is the Small Farmers' Development Programme (SFDP), administered by the Agricultural Development Bank of Nepal (ADB(N) ), which has now been running since 1975. After a promising beginning, the SFDP ran into serious difficulties with arrears and at the end of the 1980s may have been failing to reach the groups at which it was originally aimed.

The SFDP began in 1975 as an experimental outgrowth of the Asian Survey on Agrarian Reform and Rural Development (ASARRD) designed by the UN Food and Agriculture Organization and the United Nations Development Programme, Bangkok. The SFDP has subsequently been funded by the International Fund for Agricultural Development (IFAD).

---

† Reproduced with permission from ODI *Development Policy Review*, *November 1985*. The authors are, respectively, Professor at the University of Manchester Institute for Development Policy and Management and Section Officer, Institutional Division, Agricultural Development Bank of Nepal, Kathmandu.

No more suitable locale for the experiment could be imagined. Nepal, with a per capital income of US$180 in 1988, remains one of the ten poorest countries in the world.[1] Rural per capita income is well below this average; inequality of income within the rural areas is serious. Fifty per cent of the families in the rural areas receive less than 13 per cent of rural income while the top 9 per cent receive 55 per cent of the income. Landholdings average little more than one hectare, and much less than this in the hill areas where 60 per cent of the population live. Land tenure, finally, is very insecure for many people, with probably a majority of hill-land being pledged against loans in cash or in kind by private moneylenders. The SFDP was introduced initially as a pilot programme in two districts, from which base it grew to embrace, as of early 1984, 2124 schemes covering 22 698 farm families in 45 districts. This was still only a drop in the ocean of rural poverty in Nepal covering perhaps, 1 per cent of farm families, but nonetheless it is perhaps the most serious attempt so far to increase the productive potential of poor people in the country. This alone justifies a closer look at the way the scheme worked on the ground.

Small Farmer Groups vary in size from 5 to 30 members, according to guidelines laid down by the (ADB(N), the most usual size being 10 to 15 members. Groups were recruited by a Group Organizer/Action Research Fellow (GO), a graduate loan-officer of the ADB(N). On arriving in a new district the GO would conduct a 'pre-investment survey', in selected *panchayats* (the smallest administrative unit in Nepal) nominated by a district-level committee of the ADB(N), an exercise which designed to give a picture of the pattern of production and income in those localities. On the basis of this survey the GO attempted to organize informal groups of small farmers with contiguous landholdings and relatively homogeneous socio-cultural and economic status. These groups were given training, where necessary, and encouraged to embark on both personal and group projects using loan finance from the ADB(N). The size of loans was usually between Rs1000 and 50 000, that is US$60–3000 or £45–2300. Interest rates on the loans, at 11–15 per cent in the spring of 1984 according to the purpose of the loan, were well below those charged by village moneylenders. In April 1984 the ADB(N) charged 12 per cent for livestock loans and 15 per cent for crop production loans, with some reductions on these rates in the case of large loans; typical interest rates for loans from moneylenders in Dhankuta district of eastern Nepal in the same month were 37 per cent for repayment in cash and 67 per cent for repayment in kind. The group would be liable for repayment of all loans, collective and individual; each loan would be given subject to the production of a credible income-raising action plan, with no other collateral requirement. The GO, having assembled a group, would expect to participate in its meetings and to act as an intermediary between it and line agencies of the Nepalese Government, including the ADB(N), but also to help it gradually to develop self-reliance, so that after two to three years he could withdraw from participation in group activities. One GO would be expected to build up, over time, a cluster of about 50 groups in a given district; these clusters are referred to variously by the ADB(N) as sub-projects or units. As one of us has written elsewhere, the GO often had to act as 'surveyor, motivator, researcher, programmer, supervisor and co-ordinator of all small farmers in the group', and her or his role in the success of individual units was often critical.

We shall try to summarize what is known about the performance of the SFDP under three headings: effects on output and income; effects on the distribution of income; and repayment performance. Data for the SFDP as a whole are not available; we therefore have recourse to the results of case-study research carried out in different areas of Nepal by the present authors and others. We should stress that this case-study material derives from three separate investigations and not from a co-ordinated programme of research carried out by one body. It is therefore subject not only to the usual errors associated with data of this kind (such as sampling and transcription, and gaps in the respondents' memories) but also to the bias which may result from the different survey procedures not having been standardized. For this reason our data on project impact (output and income distribution) must be considered much poorer, as is usually the case, than our data on project performance (that is, repayment).

## Effects on output and income

The available data on output and income effects in the SFDP for a sample of two hill and two lowland districts suggest that:

70

**Table 1  SFDP schemes: estimated effects on output and income**

| Scheme (district) | 1975–9 Estimated impact[2] on: | | 1978–83 Estimated impact [2] on: | |
|---|---|---|---|---|
| | Average farm income and expenditure (Rs) [1] | Average grain consumption per head (kg) | Average farm income and expenditure (Rs)[1] | Average grain consumption per head (kg) |
| *Lowland* (terai) *schemes* | | | | |
| Dhanesha (Trisuli) | 1004 | 35 | | |
| Anandaban (Rupandehi) | 506 | 29 | 232 | 14 |
| *Hill-area schemes* | | | | |
| Jirikhimti (Terhathum) | | | 176 | 19 |
| Tupche (Nuwakot) | 478 | 22 | | |

*Sources:* Data for Tupche and Dhanesha schemes from Agricultural Projects Service Centre (APROSC), *Impact Study of Small Farmers' Development Project (Nuwakot and Dhanusha Districts)*, Kathmandu, February 1979. Data for Anandaban scheme from R.P. Dahal, *Income Effect on Small Farmer Households Through Expansion and Diversification of SFD Activities at Small Farmers' Development Project, Anandaban, Nepal,* Agricultural Development Bank of Nepal, January 1984.
Data for Bhirgaon scheme adapted from D.K.V. Marsh and R.P. Dahal, *Evaluation of the Small-Farmer Development Programme in the KHARDEP Area,* Agricultural Development Bank of Nepal, March 1984.

*Notes:*
1. In spring 1984, £1 sterling = 22 Nepalese rupees, US$1 = 16.5 Nepalese rupees.
2. Impact is measured as: difference between average value of farm income (or grain consumption) among SFDP participants and value of that variable in a control sample of non-SFDP participants over the stated period. The control sample is selected so as to have, on average, equivalent size of holdings, soil type and animals per holding as the sample of SFDP members.

○ the effects of the scheme on farm output and income were generally positive;
○ these positive effects may have been greater in lowland than in hill areas;
○ the positive effects may have dropped off over time;
○ the last effect may have been the consequence of a decline in the average quality of loan supervision and an increase in the difficulty of reaching small-farmer groups, as the SFDP expanded. Tupche and Dhanesha (west of Kathmandu) were the pilot projects for the entire SFDP and

were generously staffed with four GOs for a total of 1265 farm families, or 316 families per GO; each GO had two full-time assistants and a clerk to help him. By contrast, in Anandaban (in the plains) one GO had to deal with 765 families with one full-time assistant. In Jirikhimti (eastern Nepal) one GO dealt with 278 farm families with one full-time assistant and a clerk, but the quality of supervision was nonetheless poor, with only 66 per cent of loans having been supervised after disbursement. All the farm families in Tupche and Dhanesha, moreover, lived close to an all-weather road leading to the country's main market in Kathmandu. In Anandaban about two-thirds of farm families lived more than a day's walk from the main road, and all families in Jirikhimti lived more than a day's walk from any road. Understandably, the first SFDP projects were set up close to district headquarters and where possible close to all-weather roads as well but, in 1984, there were still very few of the latter in Nepal, and as the SFDP expanded into remoter areas, the average costs of transport to market rose and hence the rate of return on those projects which depended on a market outside the project area (such as horticulture, handicrafts, and many crops and livestock products) began to fall.

## Effects on income distribution

The SFDP, like other projects in the ASARRD programme, was intended quite explicitly to reduce inequality in the distribution of income. To this end, GOs were expected to confine group membership to small farmers, defined as persons whose main or only occupation was agriculture or animal husbandry, whose landholdings were less than 0.75 hectares or irrigated land or 1.5 hectares of rain-fed land and whose cash income did not exceed Rs950 (about £45) per annum. However, such data as we have belie the impression that SFDP credit was confined to, or indeed normally went to, the relatively underprivileged within rural communities. The only really trustworthy data we have are those for four eastern hill districts. These suggest that SFDP members had average landholdings half as large again as the average for the sub-districts from which the sample was drawn; the poorest farmers of all, the landless and near-landless with holdings of less than 0.5 hectares, had very little representation within

72

the SFDP, whereas 27 per cent of SFDP members owned land in excess of the 1.5 hectares which was the official ceiling for classification as a small farmer. The same proportion, 27 per cent, were above the income ceiling for the programme. Similarly literacy rates were much higher among SFDP members than among non-members, although this comparison was distorted by the fact that most SFDP groups consist exclusively of men, and literacy is very much higher among men than among women. Finally, 83 per cent of sample farmers had previously received loans (usually from moneylenders); thus the SFDP was in large measure moving people from one sector of the capital market to another, rather than tapping a new sector. These data, taken together, suggest that the SFDP did not in practice match up to the frequently encountered rhetoric which projected it as an organization which assisted the poorest groups in rural Nepal. (for examples of this rhetoric see Bhasin and Malik (1982) and the essay by Clark in Commonwealth Secretariat (1982)). At the same time, although it may have done little for the *poorest*, it did a great deal for the *poor* — the 'mean' SFDP member, with landholdings around 1.25 hectares and household income under Rs1000, could not be described as prosperous even by Nepalese standards. Whether what it achieved should be described as an improvement in income distribution is ultimately a subjective question, but the majority of observers would probably accept it as such.

The tendency of the SFDP to attract medium-sized rather than genuinely small farmers was not difficult to explain:

○ The circumstances in which the GO was expected to carry out the pre-investment survey precluded him from obtaining any meaningful data on farmers' incomes. He was expected to obtain no less than 43 pieces of information for an entire *panchayat* (about 1000 families, or 6000–7000 people) within the space of one month. Those who have done this kind of field research know this is a ludicrous request, and that 12 months, plus a further three months for recording and analysis of data, is a bare minimum for obtaining meaningful income and expenditure figures, with first-class clerical or computing resources, on a sample of 200 farm families, or about one-fifth the number in an average *panchayat*. In 1984, ADB(N) procedures, therefore, were an invitation to the GO to fabricate whatever figures he pleased if that was going to get a group formed sooner, since it was ultimately by the speed with which successful groups were formed that GOs were judged, and not by the accuracy of their figures, which nobody would be able to prove right or wrong. GOs, therefore, were impelled by bureaucratic imperatives to cut statistical corners in order to meet their target for groups formed per time period.

○ Groups, ultimately, are self-selecting. Although the GO might nominate individuals for membership of a particular group, he could not stop them refusing to accept nominees, and this is frequently what happened. Those most often refused membership were those least likely to repay their share of group loans, since if any group member defaulted on her or his share of a loan the other members had to stump up the balance before any new loan was disbursed. And, sadly, those least likely to repay their share of group loans were the poorest, since they had no reserves to draw on if their usual source of income let them down. We conclude that there were forces at work among both GOs and groups which made it exceptionally difficult to focus the SFDP on the poorest farmers.

**Repayment performance**

As the SFDP expanded, arrears on loans made under the scheme accelerated at an alarming rate. Within the scheme as a whole, the amount overdue increased by 65 per cent in the financial year up to July 1984 alone, and there were indications that the rate of delinquency increased as the scheme developed. The risk of default rose as the SFDP penetrated down the income scale towards the very poor. This is probably because if the very poor are struck by unexpected misfortune, such as crop failure or the death of an animal, they have no reserves on which they can draw to keep up repayments on a loan.

**Possible modifications**

Although, by Nepalese relative standards, the SFDP was a success in raising incomes among poor rural farmers, it scarcely touched the poorest at all, and its arrears rates over the first nine years rose to the point where it was in no sense self-sustaining and could only be kept going by repeated transfusions of overseas aid. This is a matter for particular concern in a country where overseas aid already accounts for 60 per cent of the government's development budget — and for 6 per cent of gross national product.

What could have been done to make the SFDP work better? Part of the problem, it should be clear, lay outside the agency which provided the credit. The SFDP would have worked better if some activities which were supposed to be provided in parallel with the programme's credit, such as veterinary and agricultural extension services and market information for handicraft groups, actually had been provided. In what follows we however, shall confine ourselves to those policy measures which could have been implemented directly by the ADB(N).

Three measures of reform would appear to be highly desirable:

1. A shift of some of the ADB(N)'s resources from disbursement to supervision. Our survey indicated three areas in which the supervision effort was in particular need of improvement.

○ *The pre-investment survey*, which stood as an invitation to the compilation of meaningless information. It needed either to be simplified into a 'rapid rural appraisal'-type exercise, with the implication that the rigid maximum income and landholding conditions probably would not be met, or to be carried out by proper survey methods, with the implication that there would be long delays before disbursement proper could begin and that the whole rate of disbursement would be slowed down. This was a matter on which the ADB(N) should have taken an early policy decision: if it put greater weight on income creation and speed of disbursement it would have done the former, and if it put greater weight on the distributional objectives of the SFDP it would have done the latter. Nine years into the programme it had the worst of both worlds.

○ The *screening of loans* before money was disbursed. In the early years, once a group was formed, all applications for small loans tended to go through on the nod, with the result that a large quantity of SFDP resources got devoted to activities which had little prospect of paying for themselves, in particular the servicing of outstanding loans.

○ *Post-loan supervision.* Marsh and Dahal reported that in the eastern hill districts: 'The frequency of regular follow-up supervision seems to be low. Even when there are serious problems with loan activities there is little evidence of increased supervision by SFDP'.[2] The connection between supervision levels and repayment performance, established by Maharjan and Dahal, does not need to be laboured.

2. The adoption of compulsory savings schemes. In the beginning, GOs were instructed to encourage groups to form savings funds, the proceeds from which were deposited either with the local SFDP office or in a local bank. In practice they were not always successful in this — in the Kosi Hills area (in eastern Nepal) only 27 per cent of all small-farmer groups saved regularly; sometimes, indeed, they were even unable to explain to group members that a savings scheme was creating the impression that it was a form of government tax. It seems very clear that the ability to repay group loans correlated with the possession of group cash reserves and that disbursement of SFDP loans should have been made contingent on the existence of a group savings scheme, instead of being vaguely encouraged as in the early years of the scheme.

3. Crop and livestock insurance. In the original (1976) draft documents for the SFDP, IFAD recommended the introduction of livestock insurance schemes by GOs, but no detailed plans were drawn up by them or by anyone else, and only one (voluntary) scheme in Morang in the eastern Terai had been set up by 1983. Certainly, in the almost universal absence of proper veterinary services, the most obvious way of dealing with the most frequently cited cause of loan default, namely crop failure and deaths of livestock, would appear to be compulsory insurance against these contingencies. Payment of an insurance premium, of course, constitutes an additional burden on the budget of very poor farmers; this problem could, however, have been mitigated by apportioning premium payments pro rata according to income amongst group members. The introduction of such a measure would probably not be popular in many rural communities of Nepal; but it appears to us to be a necessary measure if the problem of loan delinquency is to be prevented from constraining and ultimately shackling the growth of highly promising schemes, such as the SFDP.

# 7 Philippines: no schooling, no project

*Sometimes life is onerous, sometimes life's not fair. And sometimes, we just don't care.* Filipino song

THE NEW YORK based UN Development Fund for Women (UNIFEM) finances practical projects that help women, especially the poorest, in developing countries (see Chapter 2). So I asked UNIFEM if they could suggest a project I might visit that would demonstrate how one of their projects was reaching the poorest. They recommended the Production, Processing and Marketing of Root Crops by Rural Women in the Philippines. I visited the project in the hope that I would be able to include it in the section of this book about projects that are succeeding. Reluctantly, because the project has many good features, I have to include this in the category of projects that are not at present reaching the very poorest because of institutional factors. Those factors are, however, capable of being changed at a local level, which gives the project considerable potential.

Launched in October 1988, the three-year project lends money, without collateral, to groups of women, each 25 strong, in 8 *barangays* (villages) to help them process arrowroot and other root crops. This adds value to their crops and increases their incomes. As the project's name suggests, this is the chief aim. But when I visited the project, quite close to its half-way stage, some two-thirds of the money loaned had gone to help women with an ancillary activity, pig fattening. This is not to imply that the project had lost its way; there is a connection between pig fattening and root-crop processing.

The US$65 000 project builds on an earlier one which supported an arrowroot project in two *barangays*. (UNIFEM has contributed US$50 000 of the funding and the Filipino

77

Government US$15 000.) Root crops grow well in most parts of the Philippines — in flat country or hilly, under coconut trees, in backyards, on virtually any piece of land. Arrowroot makes a good intercrop and needs only a little rain or maintenance: 'It's a plant-and-forget crop', said a project official.

But many farmers have dropped the practice of planting arrowroot. There is very little demand for it as a tuber in its freshly harvested state and farmers do not know how to process it. 'Farm producers do not give much attention to root-crops', says a project document, 'because they do not realize the money earning potential.'[1] It goes on to say that they lack the proper know-how and skills to process the crops. Training is therefore a key part of the project.

Arrowroot flour has a number of different uses, such as biscuits, bread and cakes, and the demand for it is high. Women can either set up a small bakery to make cookies themselves or they can sell the arrowroot flour to existing bakers. Processing therefore seems to make a great deal of sense. The project was planned by the government's Agricultural Training Institute and is implemented by the Rural Improvement Clubs (RIC) of the Philippines, a non-governmental organization (NGO) established over 50 years ago to help rural women. The RIC suggested which *barangays* the project should cover and selected the women who were to be included.

The women received the credit at 12 per cent annual rate of interest and normally repay within six months. Some use the money for equipment, some to buy seeds and fertilizers, and to help them prepare their land. Most loans have been repaid on time, although the drought of late 1989 caused severe crop damage in some *barangays* and meant that repayment periods had to be lengthened.

*Barangays* selected for inclusion are in the regions of Batangas, Marinduque, Pampanga and Pangasinan. Like most *barangays* in the Philippines the selected eight are poor, although some are much poorer than others. Government figures suggest that over two-thirds of rural families are below the offically defined poverty line.[2]

Whilst some equipment is purchased by groups as a whole, the women divide themselves into sub-groups of five. Most of the women included in the project are young mothers in their twenties and early thirties, although a few are older.

They take out loans from the project as individuals but all five members of the sub-group to which they belong are responsible for repayment. Before anyone takes out a loan, she discusses it with her four colleagues and only goes ahead if the others agree. This arrangement seems to work well, encouraging good team work. A possible defaulter may be helped out of difficulties by her colleagues who know they will have to foot the bill if anything goes wrong. This kind of group guarantee is the effective collateral. In many cases the five women work together.

When women in the *barangay* of Sepung Bulaon, in the Pampagna region, heard that their village was to be included in the project, over 100 asked to join. The 25 eventually selected were from lower-income groups, say project officials, and the *barangay* was allocated around 85 000 pesos (just under US$4000) from the project.

One sub-group of five women in the *barangay* demonstrates the way the women included have seized their opportunity. With credit from the project they bought an arrowroot press, a heavy concrete contraption with a wooden handle, that presses the root crops and separates the flour from the fibre. Without the machine the women would have to pound the arrowroot by hand, a long laborious business which would probably deter them.

When the women have extracted the flour they add water, leave it to stand for several hours, drain off the water, add new water and repeat over a two-day period, by which time the flour is whiter and more acceptable for biscuit-making. The flour is laid out to dry and then taken to an adjoining bakery for turning into biscuits, or cookies, as they call them locally. Here the women use two methods of cooking: a traditional stove method which takes about 30 minutes, and an electric cooker which takes about half the time. The group bought the electric cooker out of profits. Helped by the training they have received under the project, the group produces a crisp cookie which is sold to local people and which gives the women a good financial return.

A member of the sub-group, Ising Sagun, was a housewife before the project began. As the group shares the baking, she works just three days a month at the bakery for which she earns about 300 pesos. And as far as she is concerned this is all 'extra' money to supplement the earnings of her small-farmer husband. But Ising Sagun derives an additional benefit from the project. All the members of her group took out a loan from the project to set up small piggeries. Ising bought and fattened two hogs for sale in the market. She sold them after four months fattening, making a profit of nearly 800 pesos. Her experience is fairly typical of other women in her group and in other five-member groups in Sepung Bulaon.

The reason the project gives the women credit for fattening pigs, explains RIC official Patricia Jimenez, is that arrowroot processing is a comparatively long-term business, whereas pig fattening is short term. Arrowroot takes between 8 and 10 months to grow. 'During the months the women are growing their arrowroot', said Pat Jimenez, 'they told us that they needed an additional income-generating activity to tide them over — and most of them opted for pigs.'

A rootcrops project that has seen most of its money go for pig fattening in its early stages is therefore not as odd as it seems. It is in fact a highly positive feature of the project that the women involved have genuinely participated in shaping the kind of loans made. A rootcrops project was flexible enough to change when the women pointed out the need for credit for complementary activities if they were to process rootcrops. And when the arrowroot has been harvested, any not required by the bakeries or for other uses can be used as a pig food.

The women grow their arrowroot in small plots, often between 0.1 and 0.5 of a hectare, but also in backyards if necessary. In Sepung Bulaon around 1.2 hectares was planted to arrowroot in 1989 (the project's first full year) and this area yielded 19 700 kg of tubers, a yield per hectare of around 16 tons. The 25 women are now planning to set up a co-operative that will help them to get a better price for their cookies. Training is given under the project to help the women to learn how co-operatives work.

If land is available to grow arrowroot, then all is well. The women of Sepung Bulaon say they cannot meet the demand for cookies from their 1989 output of the crop and are looking for more land on which to expand. It is here that they may run into the kind of problems experienced by a nearby project village, Dolories Magaland.

The women of Dolories were unable to persuade their husbands to give them any land on which to plant arrowroot. The comparatively high price of sugar in 1989 caused the sugar-growing men to feel that their fields were more profitably employed growing sugar rather than a rootcrop that would tie up the ground for 10 months. So then women tried, unsuccessfully, to grow the crop in their backyards. The soil in this *barangay* is sandy, in contrast with the clay soil of Sepung Balaon, and was unable to support the arrowroot in the dry weather conditions of 1989. So the women of this village harvested no arrowroot crop and are therefore doing no processing; but they do have their pigs! They all borrowed money to fatten pigs and are doing quite nicely from them. But in early 1990 they were given an ultimatum by project officials — take arrowroot seriously or you will have to drop out of the project.[3]

It is easy to blame the men of the *barangay* but it appears that no one warned the women of Dolories that arrowroot would not grow on their sandy soil if the weather were dry. Arrowroot was new to the *barangay* and the people could not be expected to know this. Again this is an example of the way an aid project introduces something new without asking enough questions as to whether it will work.

In the project *barangay* of C. Lichauco, in the Pangasinan region, the villagers grow sweet potato (*camote*) rather than arrowroot. But *camote* also has considerable processing potential (as illustrated) and is grown over larger areas. C. Lichauco has a population of just under a thousand people; its 146 households between them farm 98 hectares. The *barangay* does not strike the outsider as being obviously poor, most people seem reasonably nourished and well dressed. But average annual income per person is only 2000 pesos, half the official poverty-level income. Men have traditionally grown rice and maize; women grow vegetables, such as string beans and tomatoes. The project has encouraged them to expand their cultivation of *camote*, which grows well in the *barangay* — farmers have irrigated rice and, if the weather is dry, the women can water their *camote*.

Part of the loan to C. Lichauco was used by the women to buy a pedal-operated potato chipper that slices up the large *camote* roots. This was made locally by the village blacksmith. The chips are then fried, sugar and salt are added, and the processed product is sold as a snack both in the village or to bus passengers making a journey along a nearby main road. One kilo of *camote* makes 25 packets of chips, which sell for a peso a packet. The women therefore earn 25 pesos from a kilo of *camote* — eight times more than they receive for the unprocessed product.

One of the women selected in this *barangay*, Maxine Gambol, borrowed 3600 pesos to help her to plant and plough a hectare of land on which to grow *camote* in 1989. She harvested 1000kg, some of which was kept for family consumption (*camote* cannot be stored for long), some was sold in an unprocessed state, some was processed into *camote* chips and some was used to fatten her pigs, also purchased with credit from the project. Maxine's earnings are good, she says; 'the project has made a big difference to my life'.

Lulita Sardon, another of the women covered by the project in C. Lichauco, says that with the money she gets from selling her *camote* chips she buys more meat and fish and is able to give her family a better diet than previously. Most of the women who had benefited said the same. Some had used their extra earnings to improve their houses. Overall there was considerable evidence that the earnings from *camote* and pigs had improved the position of women and raised nutritional and living standards in the *barangay*.

The women are following up their initial gains by looking at the possibility of setting up a co-operative that will help them with marketing, possibly to get their *camote* to the capital, Manila, where it will fetch a much higher price than if sold locally.

Some 30 kilometres away from C. Lichauco lies the hillside village of Calitlitan, one of the poorest of the 8 project *barangays*. It has no irrigation, only upland rice is grown and harvests are modest. Villagers also grow onions, peanuts, pepper and *camote*, but yields and food consumption are low. Malnutrition is more obviously noticeable here than in most of the other *barangays*. The people covered by the project also suffered from the misfortune that the bank, to which UNIFEM had given a share of the project's fund, collapsed. Whilst insurance is expected to recover the money, it was sad that, some 18 months after the project had started, it was difficult to find any pigs in the *barangay*, let alone any root-crop processing. The villagers hoped simply they might benefit one day.

Despite such problems, in its first year the project helped many of the 200 women it covered to increase their earnings and living standards. Most people in the rural Philippines are poor, and the project has helped the poor. 'Eighty per cent of the total beneficiaries have increased their family's income', says a progress report.[4]

The women covered by the project are therefore faring well — but how do women in the *barangays* feel who were excluded from the project? A woman in one *barangay*, who was included, commented that 'women left out feel neglected and envious'. Project officials believe that the way to overcome this is to continue extending the project so that more women are included. After the women have repaid their loan, the money will be lent to another group of 25 women, either in the same or in a different *barangay*.

But the question remains — is the project helping the poorest? The project guidelines are revealing, saying that participants 'shall be selected on the basis of the following criteria:

1. at least primary school graduates;
2. with an income of about P2850 per annum (the poverty level is P4000);
3. members of local RIC chapter;
4. with a strong sense of community spirit and interest in the project.[5]

The fact that the project targets women who are well below the poverty level is admirable. The chief obstacles to the poorest women in the *barangays* being selected for inclusion in the project is the first criterion, schooling. The project guidelines also say 'only about 31 per cent of them (rural women) have had formal schooling'.[6] This means that 69 per cent of rural women have had no formal schooling and are excluded from the project. Inevitably they are poorer — their parents could not afford to send them to school, and so they are probably illiterate with a limited range of job opportunities.

The project co-ordinator, Rufina Ancheta, said the reason why participants must have formal schooling is that they have to be able to read and write in order to write cheques, fill in deposit and withdrawal forms etc. Unlike the Grameen Bank project described in Chapter 8, where the bank goes to the villages, the Philippines rootcrops project requires the women to go the bank premises to carry out their transactions. Whilst this may seem a small point, it is one of the worst aspects of the project. Differences in banking arrangements of this nature are *fundamental* to who is included and who is excluded.

83

If people have to go to the bank premises and negotiate in conditions which are unfamiliar to them, it is a great asset, and probably essential, to be literate. But if the bank comes to people and deals with them at home in small groups, the way the Grameen works, in Bangladesh, then literacy is not so important. The bank official completes the necessary paperwork under the watchful eye of all members of the group, some of whom are likely to be literate. So in Bangladesh, the illiterate, the unschooled, can be included. Illiteracy among rural women in the Philippines is around 75 per cent, and this is, of course, closely related to those who have no formal schooling.

Rufina Ancheta says that as the women sell their processed rootcrops and pigs in the towns, it is more convenient for them to bank in town, so that they can deposit money directly from sales. But a project under which the bank goes to the women would not exclude women from depositing money in the town branch should they wish to do so.

The fact that women included in this project are well below the poverty line, and at the same time still in the educated 31 per cent of rural women, shows the depths and the seriousness of the Philippines poverty problems. If we count the poorest as those with an income of below three-quarters of the country's poverty line, the poorest are included. If we count them as people with no schooling, that is, the majority of Filipino rural women, the poorest are excluded.

Rufina Ancheta has the understandable wish to see the project succeed; this seems more likely with literate rather than illiterate women, thus underlining what appears to be a dilemma of development projects: anyone running a project designed to reach the poorest wants to reach them and also wants the project to succeed. A determined attempt to reach the poorest can seem to project officials to jeopardize the 'success' of the project.

But the conflict can be more apparent than real. The literate are judged more credit-worthy, and more likely to be successful. This is, however, to underestimate the poorest. The experience of the Grameen Bank in Bangladesh shows that there is nothing about the vast majority of the poorest that makes them less likely to repay.

Reaching the poorest and running a successful project *can* be compatible. How then can projects be organized in such a way that the poorest are included? In the case of the rootcrops project this would mean not including clauses that participants must have completed primary school. It would mean taking the bank to the people in 'Grameen style' rather than the people going to the bank. Such changes would make running a project harder work.

People with schooling are more likely to be easier to deal with, have minds that have received some training, and be able to pick up ideas more quickly. Their education may have given them an awareness of the possibilities of escaping from poverty. They are 'ripe' for help from a project. Project officials can hardly be blamed for wanting to deal with them rather than with illiterate people who may be thoroughy demoralized and need some encouragement before they take part in any scheme. But then no one imagines that reaching the poorest is easy. Widening the project to include all rural women would make it more difficult to administer. It would not necessarily make it any less successful.

Rufina Ancheta says that the schooling clause in the project guidelines could be changed, and women without schooling could eventually be included. It is even possible that some of the children of illiterate parents could do the necessary paperwork. She points out that the schooling clause was drawn up locally and not demanded by UNI-FEM. The institutional constraints are therefore ones that could be removed at the local level.

The encouraging aspect of this project is that officials are aware that the illiterate are excluded and are sincere about wanting to include them, although the project's limited funding will not help. The project could yet do much to assist some of the demoralized poorest of Filipino society. Life, as the song says, may sometimes be onerous and not fair. And it is certainly true that people can become so demoralized that they cease to care; there is every reason why anti-poverty projects must try every possible means to reach those at the bottom of the economic pile.

*Improved methods of growing the local staple food, sorghum, (shown here being winnowed) are being supported in Somalia under an IFAD project.* (Photo: IFAD)

*The labour force on the Bhima Irrigation Project, both men and women, are landless peasants living in the project area. They are going to be settled on the irrigated land, but others have been displaced.* (Photo: IFAD)

# PART 3: *Lessons to be learnt?*

## 8 The Grameen Bank in Bangladesh — giving credit where it's due

PARTLY FINANCED BY the International Fund for Agricultural Development (IFAD), and therefore in the category of an official aid project, the Grameen Bank of Bangladesh is often cited as a model of how this type of aid can reach the poorest. The bank deserves the praise. It has taken banking out to the poorest, pioneered imaginative ways of involving them and it has reached people previously excluded. And while even the Grameen Bank has some way to go before it reaches many of the very poorest, many of its practices deserve replication — and are beginning to receive it.

The bank's origins date back to 1975 when Muhammad Yunus, Professor of Economics at the University of Chittagong, conducted a survey into how poor women 'lead their lives'. That survey was to lead to more clearly defined ideas of the needs of the rural poor and to open up a new and important channel to meet those needs.

'A grave situation faced those women who had stepped into the male world of earning', said Yunus. Having taken loans at high rates of interest, often to help them produce hand-made wares, the women were being forced to accept unbelievably low prices to repay their loans on time; this merely reinforced the poverty in which they lived. Many women in the villages kept clear of the moneylenders. Some of them spun cloth on someone else's loom for 25 taka (T) a day: had they owned their own loom they could have earned almost double that amount.

At the end of the survey, Yunus was left with one conclusion: 'If it were possible to bring financial capital into the hands of the poor, then there would be a chance for them to enjoy the fruits of their own labour'. But at that time, it was not possible;' there were no institutions that channelled finance to the poor other than moneylenders whose terms gave the poor no chance of making a decent living. 'Our banks were never meant to come into contact with poor people', said Yunus, 'they were established only to do business with the rich.'

So Yunus decided to start a bank with a difference, a bank for the poor. He set up the Grameen (rural) Bank project to lend money to people who were landless, had no assets and who could not prove they could repay. Beginning as an experiment in the village of Jobra in 1976, the Grameen Bank project broke all the standard rules and hallowed principles of banking, but Yunus had the feeling that if the creative assets of the poor could be realized, then loans would be repaid. His judgement was to be proved strikingly correct; the project he started has helped over 600,000 poor women and men to improve their living standards. Of wider importance is that this type of operation would seem capable of benefiting the poor in virtually every Third World country.

More than 90 per cent of Bangladesh's 109 million people live in rural areas, and land distribution is highly uneven. A 1977 survey found that a third of rural households own no land, whilst another third own less than two acres. 'About 80 per cent of the population were below the poverty line', said the survey, with unemployment widespread.

The treatment of women and men is also highly uneven. According to Yunus:

> The women of poor families live at the mercy of their men; they have all the obligations in the world but no rights, no security, no access to any activity that brings economic reward. They are considered liabilities.

But women usually have more household skills than are recognized, he believes, and those skills can be translated into producing for the market. 'Once a woman becomes an earning member of her family, her status in the family undergoes a positive change', he points out.

Rural development programmes were therefore needed to give poor women as well as men a fair chance. As there are only limited opportunities for wage employment in rural areas, programmes to help people make their living from self-employment were considered to have a crucial role to play. This meant giving people an alternative to moneylenders who often charge rates of interest of 10 per cent a month, and sometimes of 10 per cent *a day*.

People who borrowed from moneylenders, to make a product or provide a service, often found that after repaying the interest there was not enough left for a reasonable living. Many were deterred even from attempting self-employment because, once in the hands of a moneylender, they feared they would be there for life.

Yunus believes that it is important to distinguish between agricultural and rural credit:

> The landless do not all live on agriculture; but we have agricultural rather than rural banks, which specify rules and procedures that give the poor no chance. We have trapped ourselves into believing that anything other than agriculture is only trivial and peripheral.

The Grameen Bank has five main objectives:

○ to extend banking facilities to poor women and men;
○ to eliminate exploitation by moneylenders;
○ to create opportunities for self-employment among the poor;
○ to bring the disadvantaged into a structure they can understand and operate, and find socio-political and economic strength through mutual support; and
○ to turn the vicious circle of 'low income, low savings, low investment, low income' into an expanding circle of 'more income, more credit, more investment, more income'.

The bank lends only to landless people, although anyone with a cultivable land area of less than 0.4 acres is considered landless.

> Landlessness has a virtue [believes Yunus]! a life tied to the land tends to make people conservative, narrow in outlook, inward looking. Landless people, having no tie with the land, are likely to be enterprising, mobile and receptive to new ideas. Their existing condition makes them fighters.

When the project began in Jobra village, operational responsibility was assumed by the rural economics programme at Chittagong University. A commercial bank made a commitment to providing initial finance, and the ground-rules for lending were laid down and explained to the villagers. The new scheme operated successfully, and it soon spread to neighbouring villages.

At first (and until 1983), Grameen was a project rather than a recognized bank. It operated with help from the village branches of existing banks, using their buildings and staff for its activities. But in October 1983 the project evolved into a fully-fledged specialized bank in its own right. It was institutionalized as the Grameen Bank with the task of bringing credit to the poor, and so entered a new, if potentially more perilous, stage.

To obtain loans from the Grameen Bank, landless people are asked to form themselves into groups of five, to appoint a chairman and a secretary, and to meet together weekly with other five-member groups. This congregation of groups is known as a Centre; it appoints a Centre chief, who is prepared to become knowledgeable about the bank's rules, conduct the weekly meetings and make sure the rules are observed. A bank employee, trained in bank operations, is present at the meetings to answer queries and to advise and amplify on bank policy.

At the weekly Centre meetings, the would-be borrowers expand publicly on their plans and engage in dialogue with the bank, through its employee, under the watchful eyes of other villagers, which helps to keep exaggerations and misinformation to a minimum. For borrowers, the great advantage of this system is that they are not required to face what is to them a strange and hostile environment in the form of office desks and imposing bank buildings.

Group members who feel they have a sound idea can apply for a loan of up to T5000 (about US$250). No more than two members at a time can apply. The first two borrowers in the group are observed for the use to which they put the money and for the way they repay. Other group members are told that if the first borrowers do not repay, the remaining members will not receive loans; this puts the borrowers under peer pressure. After a month, providing that the first two borrowers have performed well, two other group members can then receive loans.

Again, a month later, given satisfactory performance by the other members, the fifth person in the group can obtain a loan. Later the first two borrowers can return for a second loan, and frequently do. In many groups the first loans are modest but, after putting that loan to good use, borrowers often seek a further loan for a more ambitious project.

Either individuals or groups can take out loans. 'Although there are lots of informal interlocking responsibilities', explains Yunus, 'formally only the borrower is responsible for her or his loan.' In the case of a group loan, members are responsible for repaying their share of the money borrowed.

Each group member deposits T1 a week into a Group Fund which is accumulated and operated by the group. When members receive a loan, they also pay 5 per cent of the amount received into this fund. This is explained to them as being like *mushti-chaal* (a handful of rice separated from the rice being cooked for the day's meal). They do not miss it and soon accumulate a sizeable amount as a reserve which can then be loaned to members to meet any immediate cash needs. An Emergency Fund also operates to insure members against default, death, disability or other accidents. Each borrower pays to this fund an amount equivalent to 50 per cent of the amount charged by the bank as interest on the loan.

Loans are repaid in weekly instalments, over 50 weeks, at 2 per cent of the loan amount. The interest (16 per cent, in 1988) is paid at the end, that is in the fifty-first and fifty-second weeks. In practice the borrower pays interest and deductions amounting to 24.5 per cent of the amount loaned, 13 per cent interest, plus 5 per cent Group Fund and 6.5 per cent Emergency Fund. When compared with the moneylenders annual rates of 120-3650 per cent, the attractions of the Grameen Bank are clear.

Following the success of Grameen in Jobra and surrounding villages, the Bangladesh Bank (the country's central bank) became convinced of its value, and another bank also committed funds. A proposal was drawn up to extend Grameen-type operations to Tangail district in the heart of the country, with the sponsorship of the central bank, the support of all the nationalized commercial banks and the Bangladesh Krishi (agricultural) Bank. But although almost 100 per cent of Grameen Bank loans were being repaid, the banks hesitated; more additional funding was needed from outside.

The World Bank was approached but turned down the request for funds, not least because it disliked the idea of loans being given to people who had no security to offer and who could not guarantee they could repay. IFAD was then approached, and offered an interest free loan of US$3.4 million. The Bangladesh Bank matched the IFAD loan on a 50:50 basis and the commercial banks became more willing to be involved. A Grameen Bank office was set up with support from the central bank and with Muhammad Yunus as director.

In 1980, the bank had 25 branches in Chittagong and Tangail districts; at the end of October 1983 the number had grown to 82 in five districts, having spread into the district of Rangpur, Patuakhali and Dhaka. By then 10 320 groups had been formed in 1191 villages; group members number 50 754, of whom 41 512 had borrowed money, 43 per cent of them women. Loans totalling over US$3 million had been received by people, most of whom had seen their income rise dramatically. The bank has since spread to operate on a nationwide basis.

By the end of 1989 the Grameen Bank employed 8000 people, had expanded to 713 branches and 728 812 individuals had taken out loans. Since 1976, the total amount of loans made is US$185 million, thus making it a sizeable operation (figures supplied by IFAD to the author in September 1990).

Among the landless the scheme has proved enormously popular, chiefly because the bank has met their needs and taken the trouble to go to them. 'The basic principle of the bank', Yunus had explained, 'is that people will not go to the bank; the bank will go to the people instead.' By 1989 loans had been taken out for over 300 different purposes and the range of activities supported shows that although a community may be resource-poor it is by no means lacking in a rich diversity of life and economic activity. A survey shows that loans had been made for trading purposes, for making processed goods, providing transport services, storing agricultural produce, marketing agricultural and non-agricultural goods and supplies and for different kinds of maintenance services. Less than 5 per cent of the loans were directly for agricultural purposes.

Amongst women, the most popular activities for which loans had been obtained were paddy husking (3958 in a 1981 survey); the purchase of a milch cow (2606); and cow fattening (1697). Amongst men, the purchase of a milch cow (1570 loans) and paddy husking (1512 loans) also figured prominently, but most loans were made to men for rice trading (1725); rickshaw purchase was also popular with men (1142 loans).

Lime-making, cycle repairing, weaving, pottery, mustard-oil making, goat rearing, flour trading, microphone rental and garment manufacture are all poular with borrowers as also are *zongoor*-making, betel-leaf cultivation and *chanachur* making. Most loans range from T500 to T3000, the average being T1600 (about US$70), with many group members borrowing more than once.

Borrowers are not asked to provide any collateral, or guarantee that they can repay, although items bought with a loan remain the property of the bank until the loan is repaid in full. The unique 'bottom line' of the project is that at the end of June 1988, the repayment rate on the bank loans was 98.3 per cent.[1] (By contrast the country's agricultural credit scheme which keeps to traditional banking principles has a default rate of 35 per cent!) This dispells any idea that the poor are feckless and cannot be trusted with money. But *Grameen Bank* lending has always been done on the assumption that an uneducated person is not necessarily unintelligent.

Grameen operations have proved popular because they have raised the level of income and have provided regular income, which some people did not have before they took out a loan from the bank. A study of 600 Grameen Bank borrowers selected at random in 1982 shows that average annual income in 1980, before a loan, was T1037. In 1982, after the loans, average income was T1740. After allowing for inflation, the real income of borrowers is estimated to have increased by 35 per cent in that time. For landless people, most of whom had never seen any improvement in their lives, such an increase came as an enormous blessing.

'One unmistakeable fact emerges', concludes Yunus, 'that given the support of financial capital people are capable of bringing about an incredible change in their lives.'

Women particularly seem to have benefited. Those who became earners have increased their status, lessened dependency on their husbands and improved their homes and the nutritional standards of their children. As Yunus said:

> Once a woman starts earning the initial benefit is enjoyed by the woman's children; they get clothes to wear, or start going to school. The second benefit comes to the whole family with the repair and improvement of the dwelling place.

There seem to have been no substantial problems about forming or joining a bank group. One survey found that 4 per cent of Grameen members had difficulty because big farmers criticized the scheme and tried to prevent them from joining; also that some young members were discouraged by their guardians from becoming members. The survey revealed that 94 per cent of group members attend their weekly Centre meetings regularly. Members were generally satisfied with the rules and procedures although about half believed that the 5 per cent deduction from loans for the Group Fund was too high. Some members disliked the rule that, should they leave the bank scheme, they had no claim over the money they had contributed to the fund. It was recommended in the survey that the bank should change this practice.

Although only a small proportion of bank loans go directly to agriculture, almost all have an impact on the agricultural sector. Farm wages have risen by a quarter in bank areas, and the leverage of a small number of powerful traders to force down prices for post-harvest agricultural produce has been substantially reduced. The traders who long enjoyed a monopoly over stocking such produce are forced to compete with many more small stockists from among the landless. This effectively breaks the monopoly; farmers are now receiving more realistic prices for their produce.

Collective activities are also supported by bank loans. One of the most significant of these ventures has been the purchase of 30 shallow tubewells by 856 borrowers, another a women's association rice husking mill. Such group efforts seem likely to grow.

Of key importance is that the landless, a once powerless group of people, are becoming an economic and even a political force to be reckoned with. Centre leaders are now contesting local elections. In some areas the weekly Centre meetings discuss election issues and members resolve that all vote for a particular candidate; a large block vote is therefore at stake. 'If the poor can organize themselves, then no political party can ignore them', says Yunus; 'government actions and policies will have to start tilting towards the poor.'

The bank, he believes, has exploded many myths:

> the usual beliefs that poor people are not bankable, that they cannot find something to earn an income from, that they cannot save, that they run out of ideas and profit, that the rural power structure will make sure that the bank fails, that rural society will not allow women to borrow from the bank, have all been demonstrated to be mere myths.

Poor people have come to understand the advantage of forming organizations for their own good, he points out: 'People who became frustrated, seeing themselves up against a solid wall, now see a door opened before them, revealing endless possibilities. They can now afford to dream about their future.'

The crunch question is how many of the poorest is the bank reaching in those areas where it is operating. A section on the bank in *Strategies for Alleviating Poverty in Rural Asia* says that a Grameen Bank in Tangail,

> has extended credit, on average to about 50 per cent of the households belonging to the target group in the area of its operation. The households in the target group who did not yet receive credit appear to be more among pure tenants and agricultural wage labourers rather than among other occupational groups. The agricultural labourers are about one-third of the target household groups but they are found to be only about one-tenth among the loanees. Since these people are the poorest of the poor, it appears that the Grameen Bank has not succeeded in serving the extremely poor as much as the other occupational groups. Moreover, since its loan operation has tended to remain limited to those already covered through repeat loans, which are virtually automatic subject to good repayment record, the extremely poor continue to remain outside the Grameen Bank net.[2]

This is worrying; the bank clearly still has work to do if it is to reach the poorest. Some of the problems could be overcome if each branch of the bank ensured that a certain percentage of loans was made to new borrowers, rather than those who have borrowed before. A related question is whether Grameen-type banking facilities can spread to come within reach of all the poorest in Bangladesh.

There are an estimated eight million landless families in Bangladesh and it will not be easy to bring credit to them with the money and organization that the Grameen Bank has at its disposal. 'Although the bank is expanding, it is still a small effort in eliminating poverty and unemployment', says Yunus, 'but its record clearly indicates that it may contain the seeds of great hope.'

There have been disagreements as to whether Grameen should itself expand or whether the type of facility it offers should be expanded through other banks. Writing in 'A Society of International Development: Prospectus 1984',

Muhammad Yunus said: 'One may be justifiably apprehensive about whether any bank left to itself will adopt [Grameen] bank-type programmes as an integral part of their business.'

An alternative to expanding the Grameen Bank itself would, however, be to urge existing banks to let the spirit generated by the bank to permeate their activities, with perhaps a legal requirement that the banks set up specialist sections, charged with the task of bringing credit within reach of the poorest in every part of the country.

There is a risk that with rapid expansion the bank will become too large to manage and will lose the close personal supervision which has helped to make it successful. As it grows, the Grameen Bank intends to increase its number of senior and middle-management people and try to overcome the expansion problem with a system whereby authority is delegated. The potential for other countries to 'do a Grameen' seems considerable — some of course already have their schemes — and IFAD describes the bank as a 'breakthrough' to an effective approach to rural credit for the landless. 'Credit is not just a simple facilitator of production or investment', points out Muhammad Yunus, 'it is a very powerful social, political and economic instrument, all rolled into one.' He believes the project has the potential to alter the basic precepts of aid to the rural poor.

For the many developing countries who are critically short of financial resources, the Grameen-type of operation has the advantage that it does not make any great demands on those resources. 'The bank has demonstrated', says an IFAD report, 'that with appropriate credit support, the rural poor and landless can find self-employment without any government welfare assistance.'

'The bank has provided a new dimension and greater thrust to the process of rural development of the country', said an evaluation report, 'and made a tremendous contribution towards raising the status of womenfolk in their community.'

The aid-funded Grameen Bank has proved an important means for many of the poorest in Bangladesh to lift themselves out of the worst aspects of their poverty. It does not claim to be a comprehensive national anti-poverty programme but it is a key element in wider attempts to overcome the country's severe poverty-problems. Perhaps, above all, it shows that it is actually possible for official aid to reach the poorest.

# 9 Ethiopian refugees in Sudan – from dependency to development

WHEN A BOMB dropped from a plane in Eritrea only yards away from Mohamed Salhhi Ajaj he was lucky to escape with his life. As it was, his right leg was completely blown off. That was in 1985 and Mr Ajaj did not waste a moment. Crippled and in pain though he was, Mr Ajaj summoned together his wife and six children, packed some belongings and left on a camel for the Sudan border.

After a few months at a reception centre for refugees, near the Sudanese town of Kassala, he and his family moved to the settlement at Girba, some 100 miles to the south. A bedmaker by trade he heard about a Revolving Fund for Refugees that was being run by the International Labour Office (ILO). He applied for a Sud£4000 loan (about US$180) and was successful. Mr Ajaj used the loan to buy a saw and a chisel, and also wood and ropes to make beds to sell to other people in his settlement. He now makes three beds a week from his home, charging Sud£90 each for them. His profit on each bed is a modest Sud£10. Because he is classed as a member of a 'vulnerable group', he receives food aid. With his handicap and with little money, Mr Ajaj ranks among the poorest of the poor — even in comparison with other refugees, he is poor.

Most of the world's refugees come into the poorest category. The ILO Revolving Fund was set up specifically to help Ethiopian refugees who have been in Sudan for some time. During the last 30 years people have fled into neighbouring Sudan to escape the fighting between Ethiopian government forces and liberation fronts in Tigray and Eritrea. In 1984, 1985 and again in late 1989, there was a new influx as drought and famine struck Ethiopia. The precise number of refugees is not known — many have settled spontaneously in towns and villages without registering — but estimates sug-

97

gest that in 1990 Sudan had 1.3 million refugees living alongside its own population of just over 20 million.

Overwhelmingly the refugees are concentrated in Sudan's Eastern region. There are probably 1 million refugees in this region of some 4.5 million Sudanese, many of whom have been in Sudan for over ten years. Many are unlikely ever to return home, yet their adopted home is one of the poorest regions in a resource-poor country.

Mainly desert, the Eastern region is poor in natural resources, agriculture is difficult and food output limited. Paid employment is in short supply, education and health services are often poor, water and basic essentials are limited in many areas. The overall level of rural economic development is therefore low. But despite the region's poverty, and the country's quite appalling economic problems, Sudan accepts all who seek refuge even though this puts an additional strain on already meagre resources.

The question on the minds of the Sudanese government and of the aid agencies trying to help the country cope with the influx of refugees in the early 1980s was how the newcomers could be turned from a 'problem' into a 'resource' and be helped to do a job that employed their skills. And how could their abilities be tapped to help Sudan's development as a whole?

Questions like these led the government to ask the ILO to carry out a survey into how refugees could be helped to become self-sufficient, and, in turn, help the Sudanese economy. In 1983 a programme was drawn up consisting of 16 projects to help refugees move from dependency to development.

When Ethiopians took refuge in Sudan they were, at first, very 'dependent' on others. Normally they arrived at a reception centre a few miles from the border with little or nothing, having walked perhaps for over a week. At the centres they received first aid, blankets, tents, medical treatment and food. Most of the new arrivals were women and children, many of their menfolk having been killed in the wars or having stayed behind to fight for liberation.

The arrivals stayed at reception centres for about three months and then moved to 'wage-earning settlements' where they were free to take a job. But jobs were difficult to find in a poor region, and opportunities to start a business limited, not least by lack of money.

With little money or material assets of their own, refugees are the kind of people that commercial banks do not want to know — the risk of lending are considered too great. The 1983 ILO survey found that 'lack of access to credit and initial working capital is the major impediment for refugees to start individual enterprises, joint ventures or cooperative activities'.[1]

A refugee may have carpentry skills and like to make furniture to sell to people in her or his area. But the basic tools of the trade and a reasonable quantity of wood are needed to get started. Unless the refugee can borrow money then she or he will have to forget the idea and continue being dependent on others.

Credit has shown it can play an important role in helping small-scale businesses to develop. One of the projects recommended by the 1983 survey was, therefore, the setting up of a Revolving Fund that would lend money to refugees without collateral to help them start an income-generating activity and provide that all-important economic breakthrough. Launched in 1985 the fund began to lend money the following year. With the ILO providing administration, the Federal Republic of Germany (FRG) provided US$0.92 million for the 1986-8 period. For the Revolving Fund's second phase, from 1988 to 1990, the FRG contributed US$2.26 million and the European Community 300 000 ecus (about US$256 000). In addition, in June 1989, the UN International Conference on Assistance to Refugees in Africa (ICAR) agreed to give Sudan US$268 300 for projects to help refugees and Sudanese women, US$160 123 to be handled by the Revolving Fund.

By the end of 1989 the fund had lent Sud£4.4 million (about US$1m) to just over 400 projects. Over four-fifths of these loans went to people who had organzied themselves into small groups; some had gone to co-operatives and some to individuals. Rates of return on these loans are high. A survey of the first 103 projects that were funded found a rate of return to the borrower on the capital she or he employed of 212 per cent.

ILO official, Azita Berar said:

There was strong scepticism when the project started. It was said that, without collateral, people would not repay their loans. But the repayment rate is over 95 per cent — and some of the

99

failures have been because people could not get materials.[2]

Sudan's severe foreign debt crisis has led to very serious shortages of foreign exchange to buy imports, which in turn led to shortages of spare parts, and to lay-offs and disruptions to the production process. It also led to businesses experiencing often acute problems getting raw materials.

Shortages of goods and lax monetary policy are among the factors causing inflation to soar: prices have been rising officially by 80 per cent a year; unofficially the figure has been closer to 200 per cent. The effect on Sudanese people of the grim economic situation has been a sharp deterioration in living conditions.

Refugees who start a business are likely to have problems both in getting supplies and in finding markets for their products. There is also very little petrol available in the Eastern region which adds to the difficulties for people who are trying to buy and sell. The result is that most businesses operate at well below their full capacity. It is hard to conceive of a harsher economic situation for any development project to operate and for anyone, especially the poor, to borrow money and use it profitably. Everything that mitigates against the launching of new businesses seems to be there.

From the start the fund's managers decided to try to help develop the refugee areas as a whole rather than just lend money to refugees. Sudanese people in the villages close to refugee settlements were also made eligible for loans and were encouraged to apply, provided they satisfied the same criteria as the refugees — that they were poor but had a skill. The fund therefore recognized that it is little use helping refugees to improve their livelihoods if that puts in jeopardy the livelihoods of Sudanese. This decision also helped to offset any local hostility to the fund.

Most of the people who have applied to the Revolving Fund for loans are poor, illiterate, landless and with few if any savings: 'Some of the people who have received loans came over the border with nothing but a shirt and a pair of shorts', said the fund's co-ordinator, Faisal Sayed Ali.[3]

What the borrowers do have is a skill and the potential to put that skill to use, given financial support. Loans made by the fund have ranged from Sud£1000–Sud£41 000. Repayment periods vary from four months to five years, depending on circumstances. By the end of June 1989, the average loan was Sud£11 585. Money has been borrowed for a wide range of purposes including mechanical and repair workshops, spinning and weaving, tailoring, brickmaking, carpentry, cereal grinding, cheesemaking, sheep raising, poultry farming, water transport and shoemaking.

Credit was initially provided at an annual rate of only 3 per cent but this was later raised to 10 per cent and then to 15 per cent from January 1990. The higher rates mean that more money is available to 'revolve' to other refugees and low-income Sudanese seeking loans. The 15 per cent rate is still much lower than the rate charged by moneylenders (normally over 60 per cent) and well below Sudan's rate of inflation, and therefore considered a bargain. Some loans have gone to refugees who are already running a fledgling business.

'The poor and the poorest of the poor among the target groups . . . have benefited from the loans', says the ILO Progress Report on the project for the half-year period ending December 1988; 'the project has taken care to assist the most disadvantaged sections of the refugees and Sudanese.'[4]

On Tawawa settlement, for example, the largest in the region, close to the town of Gedaref, over 20 people have received loans from the Revolving Fund. 'The loans have been given to the most needy people and have changed their lives', says settlement manager Klifa Mohomud Hamid. They have also contributed to a higher level of economic development in Tawawa; the need for this can be seen from the figures. Officially the settlement has a population of 13 000; unofficial estimates put the figure at over 20 000; these people share two water wells and one school between them.

When someone wants a loan she or he applies to the local extension officer on the project (there are eight of these officers, one for each region into which the project is divided). The extension officer then does some vetting and screening; this includes contacting the elders in the applicant's community and talking with local officials of Sudan's Commissioner for Refugees' office.

'An extension officer on the Revolving Fund project is a complete banking unit', said Faisal Ali. 'He vets applications, helps those who are successful to procure equipment, monitors their project and is responsible for the recovery of the money.' As loans are now increasing to the point where extension officers are finding it difficult to cope, the fund is considering employing field agents, maybe part time, as assistants to the extension staff.

Chronic shortages of fuel and spare parts for vehicles often hinder the extension staff when they want to visit applicants. Inevitably this slows down progress. Most of the refugees who have obtained loans from the fund live in settlements, either rural or semi-urban. They are not, however, excluded if they move into the towns and villages and live alongside the Sudanese. So far about 74 per cent of loans have gone to refugees and 26 per cent to Sudanese nationals.

Extension officers look at whether applicants have the necessary skills for their intended projects, or could upgrade their skills with training; they consider whether adequate supplies would be available for the enterprise and whether there will be a market for the end-product.

If the extension officer for the region is convinced that an application should be considered further, he prepares a feasibility study and presents it to one of two Revolving Fund committees: there is one for the Eastern region and one for the Khartoum region (where over 60 000 Ethiopian refugees are estimated to be living). Each of these committees has seven members including representatives of the Government of Sudan, ILO, the United Nations High Commissioner for Refugees, and the beneficiaries themselves. When a loan is approved the money is handled by the extension officer who goes to the market with the borrower(s) to buy what is needed. The officer makes the payment — it is not normal for money to be given directly to applicants. Some applicants are loaned a smaller amount than they requested. If applicants can afford it then it is suggested they make a personal contribution to their proposed venture, perhaps 10 per cent of the loan.

If refugees have no skills, they are excluded from the Revolving Fund. But the fund has a small training component to teach the skills needed to undertake a particular activity. This programme has a number of different arms. Refugees might be enrolled at a local training institute to either learn or upgrade a skill; 160 people have so far received skills training. As businesses need to keep books, training in bookkeeping and accountancy is given at the Co-operative Institute in Kassala, one of the Eastern region's main towns.

The institute was established with ILO help, and refugees come to it from all over the region. Training courses are also held in Khartoum.

Refugees who borrow are helped with buying and selling problems. The project's production and marketing unit tries to identify and overcome problems, helping people to pinpoint where they can find supplies and where they can sell their goods. It advises on the most appropriate technology to use. In the first six months of 1989, for example, the unit helped to secure a regular supply of materials for the fund's 13 shoemaking and 11 spinning and weaving projects. It helped to buy machines, equipment and tools needed by the beneficiaries, and to obtain spare parts.

What is clear is that, despite the difficult economic background, many people who have borrowed from the Revolving Fund have increased their incomes substantially. A survey of the first 103 projects financed found that the monthly income of the average beneficiary before their project started was Sud£514; but with the loan, average income jumped to Sud£1604.

The fund has helped those who have borrowed money, the people in refugee areas in general and the Sudanese economy. It has improved the availability of goods such as cooking oil, eggs, cheese, water, bread, soup powder, shoes and a wide range of clothes, handicrafts and furniture. It has increased the chances of having motor vehicles and electrical equipment repaired. Some people who have borrowed money have employed others, again helping the local economy. At least one project has stimulated house-building, creating jobs and social benefits. And the credit has enabled some refugees to impart their skills to others.

There have been other important spin-offs: businesses financed by the Revolving Fund buy materials from enterprises that are not connected with the fund, thus stimulating other industries; there are social benefits, difficult to quantify; even scarce foreign exchange might have been saved.

The projects benefit the refugees and Sudan as a whole; anything extra the projects make could be something less the country does not have to import. If we make more cheese, for example, that means a little less pressure to import cheese. (Faisal Ali in conversation with the author, December 1989.)

The story of the ILO Revolving Fund is one of people with little or no money seizing the opportunities and taking full advantage of the credit they secured. Its limitation is that it has been able to meet only a tiny proportion of requests — the fund has had only enough money to say 'yes' to 1 in every 40 applicants. By the end of 1989 it had received almost 16 000 applicants for loans, but passed only 400.

'Because of limited funding we have sarcely touched the fringe of the demand,' admitted project manager, Narayanan Kutty; 'the fund is under-capitalized — it could handle twice as many loans with only a small increase in costs'.[5]

The fund has the serious drawback that it helps only refugees with a skill, with only a limited amount of training available to help those without skills. Inevitably some of the very poorest refugees are unskilled and cannot secure a place on a training course. To reach people without money or skills a much larger fund is needed, together with more training facilities and probably a closer network of extension personnel who can get alongside the poor and find out the kind of income-generating activity that would be most appropriate.

The fund's administrative costs are high: if the commercial rate of exchange (US$1 = Sud£12.2) is taken, then the fund has lent only US$360 000. The Sudanese Government insists that aid agencies convert US dollars into Sudanese pounds at the rate of US$1 to Sud£4.4, little more than one-third of the tourist rate. At this rate of exchange the fund lent US$1 million to the end of 1989, still small compared with only US$2 million that the fund had available to it.

But getting aid through to the poorest is relatively new; making sure that the structure is right was never likely to come cheap. What the fund will need to show in the early 1990s, however, is sharply lower costs compared to amounts disbursed.

By banking on the poor, the Revolving Fund has achieved a repayment rate that any bank might envy. Up to September 1989, Sud£3 287 290 had been disbursed by the fund to 292 projects. Of this, Sud£771 023 was due to be repaid by that date, of which Sud£735 387 had been repaid — a repayment rate of 95.37 per cent — and was available for 'revolving' to other applicants. This rate of repayment is in line with funds in other countries that lend to the poor without collateral and further disproves any notion that the poorest are a bad risk.

The number of people who have applied for credit shows how this type of aid is welcomed by resource-poor communities.

Faisal Ali was optimistic that 1990 would see a big expansion in the number of projects funded, and was hoping to have 1500 projects by the end of that year.

Even with limited money at its disposal, the fund has enabled many refugees to have their own business and to generate an income and has helped towards restoring their self-esteem. The 400 projects are estimated to be benefiting around 6 000 refugees and dependants. At the end of 1990 the Revolving Fund came to the end of its second three-year phase and the last under its present organization. Foreign aid to the fund then comes to an end and a new national institution will take over, from January 1991, that will be fully managed and run by Sudanese and refugees, jointly.

The fund has shown a way in which official aid can get through to some of the very poorest peoples. 'The ILO Income Generating Project for Refugees has demonstrated the effectiveness of the Revolving Fund approach and presented a successful model hitherto non-existent in Sudan', says an ILO Progress Report.[6]

There are signs that other organizations working in Sudan are picking up the idea. The United Nations Development Programme, for example, has agreed in principle to finance a revolving fund for small-scale income and employment-generating activities for refugee and Sudanese women under the management of the ILO project.


## Saving time with a mill in Gambia

'The mill? We never expected anything like this. It's one of the best things that has ever happend to us.' A member of a women's group in the Gambian village of Njau was expressing how she felt about a milling machine that grinds the coarse grain, millet, into the flour which serves as the inhabitants' staple food.

Turning millet into flour is a job that African women do traditionally by hand pounding — and that often means around four hours of hard, hand-blistering work a day. And that is just part of a woman's day. Before pounding the millet into flour, women thresh the grain, separating the millet from the stalk, for about two hours, and then remove the husks, another hour's work at least. Some seven hours work is needed. Many women work 16–18 hours a day, seven days a week, every day. They might reasonably be classed as among the world's poorest.

Under a project funded by UNIFEM, 15 villages in Gambia have been supplied with milling machines. Now, instead of pounding their millet by hand, the women take it to the shed that houses the milling machine and leave it for trained operators to grind. The machine grinds the millet in five minutes. The women pay about a cent per kilo for the service, and save four hours a day. This saving of time is viewed by the women with delight and astonishment. So popular are the mills that women from villages without one are walking miles each day to bring their millet, locally known as *coos*, to village with mills. Women from 23 villages are making use of the mill in one of the villages.

The women said that one of the chief benefits of the mill is the way they feel — 'both healthier and younger', said one. Some of the time they save, the women use to relax and spend with their children; some of it they use to grow more food. One woman explained that the energy she would have put into pounding she now puts into the fields, weeding more and growing more. She has planted maize and beans, some of which she sells and which have given her a cash income for the first time in her life. A 'traditional birth attendant' stressed a further health aspect: 'Before the mill, heavily pregnant women would go to the field and weed, and it was too much for them; there were a lot of birth complications. Since the mill came, I have had far fewer complications to cope with.'

Communities which receive the mills pay back to UNIFEM, over a five-year period, an amount equivalent to their cost. This is then available for use in a revolving way for other villages; or communities can apply to keep the funds to purchase additional machinery. Each mill is managed by a village management committee.

The project cannot help women in landless families who have no millet to bring to a mill for grinding and who could be classed as the very poorest. But it is helping women who were previously grossly overworked and might also be classed among the poorest.

## Consulting the people in Lesotho

An IFAD official, Phrang Roy, took a long hard look at development projects in southern Africa's Kingdom of Lesotho and concluded that a fundamental cause of failure was 'the often hasty introduction of schemes without due consultation with the intended beneficiaries'.

Phrang Roy decided to travel from village to village in the Quthing district, one of the country's poorest, with two local consultants. Their aim was to discover the people's problems and real needs. Roy says that he found 'considerable mistrust' of outside development efforts. But after two years of listening to local people a project was formulated, the Local Initiatives Support Project (LISP), which is based directly on locally expressed needs and aspirations.

Funded by IFAD and the Lesotho Government, the US$8 million project aims to support what local people are doing and encourage activities that will help them overcome their problems. The consultants found that a vital aspect of rural life in Quthing district is that although most people earn their living on the land they cannot survive on agriculture alone. Landholdings are generally small and, for many rural families, the actual growing of food only accounts for about a fifth of their incomes.

'In order to meet their essential food and cash requirements', said Roy, 'the rural poor develop "coping" strategies, which piece together a patchwork of activiites.' They often show 'great ingenuity', he said, in developing and sustaining a range of non-farm activities which they switch to as circumstances dictate, activities such as brickmaking, handicrafts, petty trading, repair work, sowing and knitting.

The project is enabling people to form groups that will help make non-farm activities more profitable, also assisting with measures to improve crop productivity, to plant fruit trees (both for their fruit and to halt soil erosion), to rehabilitate community gardens and install water supplies. 'LISP is trying to enhance the effectiveness of the rural poor's coping strategies', according to Phrang Roy.

Between 1985 and 1988 some 39 groups were set up (consisting of nearly 500 members) under the project, mostly for non-farm activities. LISP officials gave advice on group formation, they discussed economic options, gave technical assistance if asked, and helped to arrange credit for any equipment that might be needed. Over half of all the farming families are headed by women who often find difficulty in obtaining credit.

Whilst the project has had successes, officials admitted that it's the more articulate, more aware and pushier poor who tend to come forward to take part in the groups. They have been conscious that they needed to make a special effort to involve the very poorest in the region. 'Field staff say it's easier to work with people who are poor, but slightly better off. We train them to work with the very poor', said the project's group promoter, Jutta Werdes.

The project was also trying in other ways to involve the poorest of the poor in Quthing district. A group of 15 people in one village, identified by the chief as being among the poorest, were offered a loan of around US$4 each to hold a 'stockafele' party (a traditional way of raising money in Lesotho which takes the form of a food and beer party).

Several of the group took loans, held their parties and raised enough money for an economic activity. One is now rearing chickens, another has started a vegetable garden, another is growing tobacco for snuff. 'None of them had previously received any outside assistance', said a project official. This close identification of the poorest, leading to loans of small amounts of money, is a sensitive and important way of ensuring they benefit from development assistance.

# 10 Non-governmental organizations (NGOs): giving official aid a lift

PROJECTS FUNDED BY NGOs are often to be found in the same areas of developing countries as official aid projects. In the eastern region of Sudan, for example, where the International Labour Organization (ILO) is running its Revolving Fund for Refugees credit project, the NGOs Save the Children (US) and ACCORD both have credit schemes for refugees. The ACCORD smallholder scheme has helped around 5000 refugees and displaced peolple.

Grants by Western-based NGOs to developing countries totalled around US$3.6 billion in 1988.[1] This amount may be small in comparison to the West's official aid of nearly US$50 billion but it is nonetheless a significant sum, mostly geared to meeting the needs of the poorest. And NGOs have a part to play in giving the official aid effort a lift which goes beyond mere cash.

Although NGOs finance smaller projects than official aid agencies — projects which inevitably can reach comparatively few people — they have more chance of getting through to the poorest of the poor. They are smaller, less bureaucratic, less tied down by rigid financial criteria and employ people who are more likely to live in poor communities. NGOs have earned their reputation of getting aid through to many of the poorest. In view of this, should not more official aid be channelled through them?

Speaking specifically of multilateral aid, although his comments could also apply to the bilateral variety, Ozay Mehmet of the University of Ottawa, has argued that such aid is 'structurally inappropriate to the task of egalitarian development'.[2] He proposes that an increasing share of aid should be 'delivered *directly* to specific target groups without the intermediation of governmental organs in developing countries.'

109

Non-governmental organizations, points out Mehmet, have 'direct access to target populations. They are able to reach poor and needy groups in a direct way, cutting across red tape and bureaucracy. . .'

But would NGOs welcome such a shift of official aid resources through them? Is it fair to ask them to do it? Could they handle it?

World Bank sociology advisor, Michael Cernea:

> Observers have noted that NGOs are so frequently lost in self-admiration that they fail to see that even the strengths for which they are acclaimed can also be serious weaknesses: for instance in the face of pervasive poverty, 'small-scale' can merely mean 'insignificant'.[3]

Handling greater volumes of aid would help NGOs make a more significant impact. But would they like to do it? 'Obviously there are limits on how much additional money we could properly utilise', said the director of one aid agency. Handling official aid would mean that the NGOs might have to make changes in the way they operate, and this just might undermine their service to the poor. On the other hand, while recognizing that there are limits, many voluntary aid agencies do believe that they could, satisfactorily, handle *more* aid monies without jeopardizing their operational style.

Ronald Hodson, Chief Executive of Action Aid:

> If there was a clear understanding that funds were going to increase regularly by an agreed percentage, we could gear up and plan to utilise significantly more funds. However I suspect the maximum rate at which we could grow responsibly would be something in the order of 20 per cent per annum.[4]

Another director said his agency would be 'glad to be a channel for an increasing share of British government aid' but added that 'one limitation is the availability of additional competent experienced personnel'. Mr Paul Spray, head of aid at Christian Aid, said the agency 'could take double the £2 million a year we receive from the British government'.[5]

It seems likely that in the case of British aid, more funds will be going to NGOs through an arrangement known as the Joint Funding Scheme (JFS), under which the government gives a pound for every pound that an NGO grants to certain anti-poverty projects. The scheme, which began in 1976, seems successful. Around 50 NGOs have received funds and

110

projects launched have helped people on very low incomes, including landless peasants and destitute women. To qualify for funds from the JFS, projects must be 'developmental, not humanitarian' — a puzzling separation if the purpose of development is to benefit humankind!

One of the largest pound for pound schemes is being undertaken with Water Aid, in the eastern province of Sierra Leone. Chiefly through self-help construction schemes, the project aims to provide clean water to 70,000 people; a programme of health education is also included. Under this type of scheme at least some of the poorest people stand to gain.

The size of JFS, however, remains small. Although the Overseas Development Administration (ODA) boasts in its Twenty-fifty Anniversary Review (1989) that 'the scheme has more than quadrupled in less than five years', in fact only £16 million went to JFS in 1989 out of £1400 million in aid.[6] If NGOs came up with the right projects how much more would be available? The scheme has been scheduled to grow substantially — to £27 million in 1991 to 1992 and to £64 million in 1994 to 1995, but the JFS would then still account of less than 3 per cent of British Government aid.

A number of multilateral agencies also have joint funding schemes with NGOs but these schemes seem unlikely to play a major role in their overall aid effort, with the possible exception of the smaller agencies such as the International Fund for Agricultural Development (IFAD) and the United Nations Development Fund for Women (UNIFEM), both of whom have a more natural affinity with NGOs than the larger official agencies.

The amount of official bilateral and multilateral aid given through NGOs deserves to be at the highest levels the NGOs can handle. There are however other, and potentially more significant, ways in which they can give official aid a lift. The world of official aid can learn much from the way that at least some NGO projects are reaching the poorest.

Richard Holloway says that NGOs can 'look for alternatives to the existing government systems for delivering resources to the rural poor'. He points out that when the organizations have implemented and reinforced such alternatives, 'and they are seen to work, they must be introduced to government policymakers with the intention of having them integrated with reformed government programmes'.[7]

An organization that is running a project which demonstrates how well the poorest respond, when given a particular development opportunity, can help to remove government mistrust of the poor. Governments and aid officials often need convincing that the poor can profitably employ any money loaned or given to them. The work of NGOs can help towards that conviction. They can pioneer new and imaginative ways of reaching the poor from which governments can learn. Not every kind of work done by NGOs is suitable for being copied by governments. Helping people to organize, for example, is not usually a government activity. But there are important possibilities for replication.

NGOs can also persuade governments to modify programmes by pointing out inconsistencies and by doing research into alternative ways of implementing programmes. And they also 'help governments think differently, act differently,' said Holloway. He tells of how aid advisors in Indonesia are 'often frustrated by the inflexibility of government machinery' and have turned to Indonesian NGOs for 'fresh ideas and experience'.[8]

Official aid agencies, genuinely trying to reach the poorest, are likely to find that involving NGOs in project design makes good sense. The NGOs have the opportunity to see that the project is designed so the interests of the voiceless poorest are defended and promoted; they can serve as a bridge between them and official aid: 'No NGO should seek to organize a big project,' believes Robin Poulton, 'but no major donor should fund such a project unless the NGOs are included in the project design.'[9]

An NGO can suggest that it partners government in running a particular project. But Holloway warns of the danger that government may not so much learn from NGOs as try to get them to run projects 'government-style' with insufficient attention to essential local detail.[10]

Official aid agencies can learn from the way that NGO staff live and work. NGO personnel are more likely to live locally, take the trouble to understand local people and the way they work, and find out what they want. When official aid agency workers do this it can pay big dividends, as witness the case of the IFAD official in Lesotho, (see Chapter 9). Official aid personnel have rightly come in for a great deal of criticism for being the 'lords of poverty'. If they really are to help the poor, they have to be prepared to live among them and try to understand them. This is especially crucial during a project's design stage. Official aid projects would then have a better chance of being drawn upon a more informed and sensitive basis.

Again NGOs can play an important publicity role, highlighting weaknesses of existing official policies and stimulating debate about alternatives. Ronald Hodson says that Action Aid 'has chosen to try to monitor and publicise the successes and failures of the British aid programme'. Paul Spray believes that NGOs on the ground can fight back against 'the more idiotic official aid schemes' that harm the poorest, and points to the encouraging developments in Bangladesh and India.

The aid climate can also be influenced by the work of NGOs, helping make it more likely that official aid benefits the poorest. NGOs which participate in the JFS have been successful in persuading the British Government that it is an area worth expanding. As the JFS can reach the poorest this is welcome, even if the scheme is still a small proportion of overall aid.

NGOs concerned with appropriate technology have brought to the attention of donor governments the technologies that work for the neediest groups of people. Projects that employ small-scale technology are more likely to be relevant. The Intermediate Technology Development Group (ITDG) has shown that small is not only beautiful but successful. The Appropriate Technology movement is listened to by government aid policymakers, even if, in the case of Western donor governments, changes in policy have been slow to come. The 'ability to propagate new ideas and influence policymakers in government . . . is perhaps the most important intangible asset of the AT Movement', wrote Nicolas Jeqier.[11] The British Government's ODA shows signs at least of being more aware that technology supplied under an aid project must be appropriate for the task. In addition, ITDG's research into appropriate technologies has increased their availability.

A theme that has occurred many times in this book is the low level of social organization amongst the poorest communities. One of the most important ways in which NGOs  could give official aid a lift is to help the poorest to organize, to increase their own power and to be able to participate in and take advantage of official aid schemes. NGOs can help the poorest to find their own power. Stein Hansen, speaking of India:

> In areas where the rural poor have been able to form organizations and associations, they have managed to win a greater share for themselves in the benefits of growth and expansion of public infrastructure.[12]

Below, Antony Ellman shows that NGOs can help the poorest to organize so that they have a fuller understanding of what they need to do to benefit from government or other department programmes.

## Helping the poor to organize

ANTONY ELLMAN

Examples can be found all over the Third World of development projects which, though designed to help the poor, have benefited primarily the rich. Government and party officials, local leaders and wealthy villagers are expert at gaining control of such programmes while the poor, almost by definition, lack the knowledge and the organization to grasp the opportunities and retain the benefits for themselves. Thus irrigation projects in India, agricultural co-operatives in Kenya, pastoral programmes in Peru, despite the best of intentions, have often had the effect of widening rather than narrowing the gap between rich and poor.

In many countries non-government organizations (NGOs), both indigenous and international, have come to recognize that the first step towards creating sustainable development from which the poor will gain is to help poor people to organize themselves — not necessarily to fight for their rights, though in many instances an element of this is necessary, but at least to understand the procedures that must be followed for applying for bank loans, taking advantage of subsidized inputs and obtaining access to the support services and training programmes that governments or official aid agencies have set up for their benefit.

Band Aid, with the £80 million that it allocated to long-

Antony Ellman is an agriculturalist at the Commonwealth Development Corporation specialized in the planning and management of small farmer development projects. He is also Chairman of Barnes Third World Link.

term development programmes in Ethiopia, Sudan and countries of the Sahel, has worked mainly through NGOs to catalyse such action. Christian Aid's recently adopted strategy document, *To Strengthen the Poor*, aims to redress the balance of power between North and South, as well as between rich and poor in Third World societies. Many Third World NGOs concerned with rural development now see themselves as intermediaries between organizations of the poor on the one hand and governments, commercial interests or external aid agencies on the other.

One such Indian NGO is Grama Vikas, established in 1979 in Karnataka State in South India. Grama Vikas, which means village development, was formed by a retired Indian forester and his journalist son with the objective of 'relieving rural poverty and promoting social justice'. The founders believe that 'the battle against poverty can only be won when people learn to work together and plan their own development through collective action'. The role of women is seen as critical, since 'change is possible only when rural women involve themselves in decision-making and programme implementation'.

Having limited funds of its own, Grama Vikas has formed links with a number of Western donors — Oxfam, Novib, Community Action Abroad — as well as with Indian voluntary groups, which have funded training programmes, night schools, nutrition programmes, tree-planting, agricultural and livestock development activities. But Grama Vikas is very conscious of the danger of creating dependency on outside agencies. It does not look for continuous funding for these programmes but rather for seed capital which it uses to catalyse generation by village groups of revenue for reinvestment, such that the programmes become self-sustaining. In the case of larger programmes, the initial investment enables groups to gain the experience and credit-worthiness they need for seeking commercial bank loans or government assistance for later phases of the project activity.

Gramas Vikas' strategy is to help people to set up Sanghas (village associations), which then form a link with an individual donor agency. The Sangha in one village, Mallappanahally, has been connected since 1984 with a small British NGO called the Barnes Third World Link (BTWL). This link provides an interesting case study of experience in helping the poor to organize and improve their lot.

Mallappanahally is a village of 112 households, 46 families being Harijans and 42 of the Kurubas (shepherd) caste. The total landholding of the village is 302 acres; 77 acres are irrigable and the rest is rain-fed. There are 52 marginal or landless farmers who depend on agricultural labour or share-cropping for their livelihood. The village irrigation system has become badly silted up through deforestation and cultivation of the water catchment area, and the reliability of irrigation is much less than it was 20 years ago. There is a government primary school in Mallappanahally but few of the poorest families can afford the fees. There is no clinic, and the village water supply is totally inadequate.

Mallappanahally Sanga, formed in 1984, has 27 members coming mainly from marginal and landless households. There is an associated Mahila Samithi (Women's Association) with 45 members. The Sangha and Mahila Samithi correspond regularly with BTWL, discussing their programmes and priority needs, and BTWL raises small amounts of money through bazaars, concerts and members' subscriptions. So far BTWL has helped Mallappanahally Sangha to buy 1.5 acres of paddy land and 4 acres of dry land, which are farmed by the community. The men prepared the land, women plant and weed the crop, children collect manure and apply it to the fields. The proceeds from the harvest are used to fund a night school for children who are working during the day, a nutrition programme for mothers and infants, and a sheep-rearing programme for women of poor households. BTWL pays the teachers' and nutritionists' salaries, which will soon be taken over by the community. BTWL has also provided money for a revolving fund, and has helped the Sangha to purchase a pair of oxen and a cart, which are hired out to members at an economic cost.

Mallappanahally Sangha determines its own priorities and only accepts money which will help its members to become self-reliant: 'Money should not make programmes; they must develop by themselves', the secretary of the Sangha wrote in a recent letter to BTWL.

Such experiences of working together for their own advancement have had a significant impact on the members' self-confidence and ability to exploit other sources of development assistance. In 1987 Mallappanahally Sangha organized 127 individual bank loans for its members for planting fruit trees and purchase of livestock. In 1988 a group of Mahila Samithi women who had been working on a road-building programme, for which they had not been paid fully, had the courage to march to the government contractor's office and stage a sit-down until they received their dues. The Sangha has recently persuaded the district hospital to start an immunization programme for children in Mallappanahally and has taken on a contract with the Karnataka Social Forestry Programme to raise 40,000 tree seedlings for distribution in Mallappanahally and neighbouring villages. It is currently negotiating for a bank loan to sink a well and purchase a pump for groundwater irrigation of its dry land.

Even the Sangha members' children have started to take action, as illustrated by this telling case study sent by the project organizer.

## Awareness in action: a case study

'Forty-three children in Mallappanahally decided some months ago that they should earn some money on their own. They were left to themselves to think about the means. They decided to learn some devotional songs and go round from house to house in two or three villages singing these songs. They learnt the songs from teachers in the night school, practised and went round the three villages singing them.

'This was something that had never happened before. It assumed special importance in one village where most of the people are Brahmins. These Harijan children, cleanly dressed, going round singing devotional songs, some in Sanskrit, impressed the villagers most.

'The children were able to raise only Rs200(£8) in cash and kind. Nevertheless they were proud of this earning. The question arose as to what to do with the money, and how to increase it.

'They overheard the members of the Sangha discussing indebtedness in the village. One of the members jokingly said to the children, "Hey, why don't you spend the money releasing some mortgaged land?" The children said "Why not?" They asked the members of the Sangha to help them.

'With Rs80 they got a bit of land released and used the balance of the money for fertilizer and seeds. They cajoled the elders to help them in ploughing the land. The children

117

themselves did all the lighter work of transplanting, watering, harvesting and threshing. The net profit was Rs262. Though they had taken over the mortgage for two years, the children felt they had made enough profit in one crop itself, and released the land to the poor owner.

'Thus, a piece of land which had been mortgaged about ten years ago, and from which the moneylender was enjoying the produce, was restored to the original owner within one year and without him having to repay the loan.

'The offshoot of this small venture by the children was that it set the Sangha and the Mahila Samithi thinking seriously about land redemption. They came up with proposals for redeeming such mortgaged lands, and approached Oxfam and Grama Vikas for help. Such help has been obtained and the programme has now started.

'The children are happy that, out of their small effort, a larger programme resulted and their parents could redeem their mortgaged lands.'

Similar experiences have been recorded by many other NGOs working with groups of poor people in India and elsewhere. The groups depend for solidarity and sustainability on remaining small and homogeneous. When needs are identified which require more skills or resources than the members possess, their solidarity gives them a chance of extracting the necessary inputs from governments or other development agencies.

When more ambitious programmes are attempted, requiring co-operation betwen people whose interests are likely to be in conflict, a different set of problems arises. The Mysore Relief and Development Agency (MYRADA), another Indian NGO which works in Karnataka State, has for some years been promoting people's participation in watershed management. It has recognized that the short-term interests of large and small farmers are not the same. Farmers owning only dry land, usually high in the catchment area, ought to plant trees to protect the irrigation system; but having no irrigated land they do not gain personally from such action in the short run, nor can they afford to tie up all their land in trees. Farmers with irrigated land, on the other hand, see little immediate benefit in allocating resources to planting trees on other people's land.

MYRADA concludes that, while a Watershed Management Association representing the interests of all the farmers in the watershed is needed, it should not replace the smaller more homogenous Sanghas. It should maintain regular systematic contact between the different interest groups and should use its strength to pressurize government and political authorities to bring services and compensation to those who lose out in the short run in the interests of long-term benefits to the majority.

Thus at all levels in the rural community, organization of the poor and mobilization of the appropriate support services are the key to helping poor people help themselves. NGO's constitute a vital element in channelling such assistance to the poorest of the poor.

*Shoemaker Admasou Uykon is an Eritrean refugee in Sudan. He received a S£15,000 loan under the ILO Revolving Fund project, which helped him to buy equipment. This, he says, helped him to treble his output of shoes. He is a rare case; numbering among the poorest, he has benefited from an official aid project.* (Photo: John Madeley)

# PART 4: *Conclusion*

# 11 Twelve guidelines for reaching the poorest

MRS PENNY LONGHAUL and Mr Ivor Mill, highfliers in their government's overseas aid ministry, recently found themselves on the minister's carpet. The minister, a new broom not adverse to sweeping clean, had just returned from a four-country visit to Africa. Before embarking on the visit she had, like all good ministers, read very carefully the briefings prepared by her civil servants and she noted with pride what her ministry was doing to overcome poverty.

But the visit was something of a shock. She met happy people who said they were gaining from her government's aid projects, but her air-conditioned limousine did not prevent her from seeing a great deal of poverty. She began to wonder whether the poorest peoples were in fact being covered by the aid programmes for which she was responsible. The officials who publicly re-assured her about this later told her privately that something was going wrong. It was the better-off who were usually gaining, they admitted. Much of the aid was not appropriate if the poorest were to gain; enough questions were not being asked, they owned up. All of which infuriated the minister.

Longhaul and Mill were left in no doubt about their minister's feelings. 'What is the point of us having an aid programme', she wanted to know, 'unless it is aiding the poorest? Listen — I want you go to away and come back to me as soon as you can with guidelines that our aid policy must follow if the poorest are to be reached. And I want you to present it to me in basic, non-technical terms.'

Our highfliers went away, laboured long, sweated hard and poured over the evidence of the failures and successes of government aid. And after a succession of hard day's nights they came up with the following guidelines that the country's aid projects should include if the poorest are to be reached.

○ A project must devote *careful, patient and painstaking attention to detail.* The people on the ground that a project is intended to benefit must be consulted at the design stage and genuinely participate. If there is a key to successful development it lies in the participation of local people in development projects that are meant to help them. Project officials need to listen carefully and show a sensitivity to what they hear.

○ Many projects do not reach the poorest because of a failure to investigate and understand how they live their lives. As a result, too many projects are insufficiently grounded in poverty considerations. *Projects must genuinely correspond to local realities.* Only then will they win the support of local people and stand a chance of helping the poor who need help the most.

○ Our projects must *involve non-governmental organizations at the design stage* wherever possible. NGOs often have a knowledge of the poorest that is invaluable if we are to reach them.

○ The poorest often do not participate in aid projects because they are disorganized. They may have no organization through which to make their voice heard. *Training the poorest in organizational skills can form part of project design.* This is again something that might be done in cooperation with NGOs.

○ The poorest cannot afford complex and expensive technologies. And they are often not interested in nor do they care to be bothered with grandiose technologies that seem irrelevant to their experience. *Projects must ensure that technology is low cost, human scale and appropriate.* Our projects have to supply the poorest with what they are capable of using. Low-cost technologies appropriate for rain-fed agriculture are crucially important, for example, provided this is done by working with the poorest farmers to develop improved systems that are based on their own perceptions and willingess to innovate. When we support an irrigation scheme we must ensure that canals and water courses serve poor areas on an equitable basis.

○ Very low levels of rural development are responsible for a great deal of poverty. This means that the rural poorest do not earn enough to be able to buy the food and basic essentials they need. *Projects must aim to raise the level of rural development in poor communities* and must do so with bias to the poorest in mind. We must ask: 'will the poorest gain from this activity?' If not, can we suggest that a bias is built into it, in their favour?

○ It is little use running something like a small-farmer project through a local institution, such as a co-operative, that excludes from its membership all farmers who have less than a certain landholding! *Projects must carefully assess whether local institutions are suitable.* If not, special ones could be encouraged. Under an official project in Bangladesh, for example, special co-ops for landless women and men have been established.

○ Again if we are supporting health projects, *community-based health structures should be in place before new technology comes in.* Otherwise there is a danger that the technology will simply not come within their reach.

○ Because the poorest are often unschooled and illiterate this does not mean they are unintelligent. *Projects must trust the poorest.* If we want to reach them we must treat them as partners. And if we can make literacy a part of a project, this can help the poorest realize their potential.

○ Credit programmes have proved to be an excellent way of reaching the poorest. And rates of repayment on money borrowed by the poorest are usually higher than they are for money borrowed by the rich in the Western world. There is no evidence of an inherent conflict between poverty-eradication and profitability. No one should be excluded because they are very poor. *We should support more low-cost credit programmes and make sure that the local institutions that implement them do not exclude the poorest.* If they appear to do so, we must suggest changes. We must ensure that credit programmes take the bank to the people rather than the other way round, and that they be 'burglar-proofed' so that the better-off do not walk off with the benefits.

○ *Our projects must not gamble with the lives of the poorest.* If new crops are planned, for example, we must ask if the soil and climate of their area are suitable for them? We must not encourage the poorest to grow something for which there is no market. We must ensure that the market is in place beforehand.

○ We must ask *does the project have a land-reform component?* The poorest often do not own land. We need to be bolder in encouraging at least some recipient governments to take land reform more seriously, remembering that countries that have implemented land-reform programmes have seen sizeable increases in food output. People with their own land usually work it more thoroughly than if they are working someone else's.

The minister liked the guidelines but made it clear to Long-haul and Mill that there were no laurels to rest on. 'Keep adding to them, keep researching, keep looking, keep sharpening what you are saying,' she told them, 'so that we can improve our chances of reaching the poorest. More thinking needs to be done if a higher proportion of the very poorest and neediest are to be reached,' she said. 'Keep searching for new ways of tackling the problems which cope with the realities of the individual local situation and which take into account the real world of the poorest. And, in the meantime, I plan to incorporate your guidelines into our country's aid policy.'

Would that all aid and development ministers of donor aid countries were so enlightened! If aid is to reach the poorest, ministers and civil servants in aid ministries also need to show sensitivity and care.

There is much talk in development circles about the need to 'empower' the poor, to give power to people who do not have it. It is however more a question of helping the poor to empower themselves, to discover, or perhaps rediscover, their power and glimpse the hope of improved lives. When people feel they lack the means to change their situation, their interest in doing so can cease. If the aid effort can help them to release their talents and find their own power, it can make a significant contribution.

The poorest are not 'an isolated and unreachable underclass', Riddell reminds us. As he points out 'the wide diversity of characteristics' they possess means that they can be reached.[1] The examples given in these pages bear that out. The task of reaching the poorest is difficult but not impossible — and for all the difficulties it is a problem that has to be faced and worked on rather than abandoned. NGOs have an excellent record of reaching the very neediest people in the poorest communities but government and multilateral aid agencies have the major role to play.

The scale and depth of the plight of the poorest have been seen many times in this book — in Bangladesh, India, Mali, Nepal, Sudan and the Philippines. In these and in other developing countries millions of lives are daily disfigured by the pain of hunger; abilities and potential are stunted because of woefully inadequate resources. This is why the right kind of aid is necessary. Western countries can provide at least some of these resources and do so in a targetted way. The *how* of reaching the poorest is becoming clearer. There is no reason why the task should be delayed.

# Notes

## Foreword

1. Roger C. Riddell, *Foreign Aid Reconsidered*, John Hopkins/James Currey/ODI, 1987, p. 218.
2. Robert Cassen, *Does Aid Work?* Oxford University Press, 1986, p. 110.
3. OECD Report, Paris, 1985, p. 259.
4. Bernard J. Lecomte, *Project Aid: Limitations and Alternatives*, OECD, Paris, 1986, p. 74.

## Chapter 1

1. David Millwood and Helena Gezelius, *Good Aid*. SIDA, Sweden, 1985, p. 54.
2. OECD Aid Reviews, 1989, OECD, Paris. If donor countries met the UN aid target and gave 0.7 per cent of their national incomes then official aid would double. In 1989 the aid given by the 18 donor countries belonging to the OECD Development Assistance Committee represented 0.35 per cent of their national incomes, exactly half the UN target.
3. Peter Peek, *International Labour Review*, Vol. 127, No. 1, 1988, Geneva, p. 85.
4. IFAD, *Annual Report 1987*, IFAD, Rome, 1988.
5. Quoted in Riddell *op. cit.* p. 218.
6. Michael Lipton, quoted in *Fragile Coalitions: the Politics of Economic Adjustment*, Joan N. Nelson *et al.*, p. 96, paper No. 12, ODC, Washington, 1989.
7. *World Population Data Sheet*, 1989, Population Reference Bureau Inc., Washington.
8. FAO, *Agriculture: Toward 2000*, FAO, Rome, 1987.
9. Interview, Mali, March 1988.
10. Geoffrey Griffith, *Missing the Poorest*, Institute of Development Studies, Discussion Paper No. 230, May 1987, Sussex.
11. R. Chambers, *Rural Development*, Longman, 1983, p. 25.
12. Cassen, *op. cit.*, p. 110.
13. *Bangladesh: Country Study and Norwegian Aid Review*, the Chr. Michelsen Institute, Bergen, 1986, p. 179.
14. Pearson Report, *Partners in Development*, Pall Mall Press, 1969, p. 7–8.
15. Judith Hart, *Aid and Liberation*, Gollancz, 1973, p. 182.

126

16. *Cmd 6270*, HMSO, 1975.
17. *Real Aid: A Strategy for Britain*, Report of the Independent Group on British aid, 1982.
18. Paul Mosley, *Poverty-Focused Aid: The Lessons of Experience*, Action Aid, 1987, p. 4.
19. *Bangladesh: Country Study*, op. cit., p. 179.
20. Mosley *op. cit.* p. 5.
21. World Bank, *1988 Annual Report*, Washington, 1989, p. 38.
22. Peek *op. cit.*, p. 79.
23. T. Hayter and C. Watson, *Aid: Rhetoric and Reality*, Pluto Press, 1985, p. 235. Banks such as the Grameen Bank in Bangladesh are showing that the poor are not necessarily a poor risk.
24. Lecomte *op. cit.*, p. 24.
25. *Unicef*, New York, 1984.
26. Cassen *op. cit.*, p. 110.
27. P. Mosley, *Can the Poor Benefit from Aid Projects?* University of Bath, 1983, p. 25.
28. The *Economist*, 21 July 1990, p. 69.
29. Albert Berry, *The Impact of Development Projects on Poverty*, OECD, 1989.
30. *Irrigation Technology and Commericalization of Rice in the Gambia: Effects on Income and Nutrition*, IFPRI Research Report, No. 75, 1989, Washington.

## Chapter 2

1. *IFAD Annual Report, 1987*, IFAD, Rome, 1988, p. 8.
2. *IFAD Annual Report, 1982*, 1983, p. 66.
3. Private discussions with the team at IFAD's General Assembly, 1987.
4. *IFAD Annual Report, 1987*, 1988, p. 28.
5. *Ibid.*, p. 8.
6. *The Role of Rural Credit Projects in Reaching the Poor*, IFAD Study Series, Vol. 1, 1985.
7. Lecomte *op. cit.*, p. 75.
8. *IFAD Annual Report, 1983*, 1984, p. 4.
9. The projects were in Cameroon, Ethiopia, Indonesia, Lesotho, Mali (2), Nigeria, Swaziland, Tonga and Western Samoa.
10. *IFAD Annual Report, 1987*, 1988, p. 96.

## Chapter 3

1. IFAD, Project Document EB 83/19/R42, IFAD, Rome, 1983.
2. Based on information supplied by project staff, March 1988.
3. Conversation whilst visiting the project in March 1988.

## Chapter 4

1. Quoted in *India: Development and Aid. Norway's Contribution and Future Options*, Stein Hansen, Economic Research and Policy Planning, Norway, 1987, p. 79.

2. S. Guhan, 'Aid for the Poor: Performance and Possibilities in India' in *Strengthening the Poor: What Have We Learned?*, John Pleuris *et al.*, ODC, Washington; US–Third World Policy Perspective No. 10, 1988, p. 191.
3. Guhan *op. cit.*, p. 196.
4. Hansen *op. cit.*, p. 95.
5. *Ibid.*
6. *Ibid.*, p. 96.
7. Oxfam Project Paper MPD 48,67,66, Oxfam, Oxford, 1989.
8. IFAD document, Mid-term Evaluation Report of the Bhima Command Area Development Project, IFAD, Rome, 1984.
9. Hansen *op. cit.*, pp. 36–41.
10. Details of this project are drawn from Hansen *op. cit.*, pp. 101–3.
11. Mosley, *Poverty-focused aid, op. cit.*, p. 16.
12. Mosley *op. cit.*, p. 16.
13. *Ibid.*
14. Steve Percy and Mike Hall, *British Aid to India. What Price?*, Spokesman Books, 1987.
15. *Ibid.*
16. Guhan *op. cit.*, pp. 197 and 199.
17. Hansen *op. cit.*, p. 91.

# Chapter 6

1. *World Development Report*, 1983, World Bank, Washington.
2. D.K.V. Marsh and R.P. Dahal, *Evaluation of the Small-Farmer Development Programme in the KHARDEP Area*, ADB(N), March 1984, p. 21.

# Chapter 7

1. Production, Processing and Marketing of Root Crops by Rural Women. *Project Guidelines*, Agricultural Training Institute, Quezon City, Philippines, 1988, p. 1.
2. Government of the Philippines, *1985 Census of Income and Expenditure*, Manila.
3. There appears to be a big demand in Asia and the Pacific for credit to fatten pigs, some of which UNIFEM has tried to meet. Women in Tonga are among those who have borrowed money for pig fattening, but a visit to a UNIFEM-funded project revealed some surprises. It was men rather than women who were looking after the pigs. And again there were doubts as to whether the poorest were included. Out of three farms visited, one of the women borrowers was away in Australia, another was in New Zealand and the third was said to be in a nearby town. This could either show that pig fattening pays big dividends or that the women were hardly to be counted among the poorest.
4. Production, Processing and Marketing of Root Crops by Rural Women, *Progress Report*, October 1988–December 1989, Agricultural Training Institute, Quezon City, Philippines, p. 4.
5. *Ibid.*
6. *Ibid.*, p. 1.

# Chapter 8

1. IFAD Report on the Grameen Bank, AB89/36/P10/Rev. 1, April 1989.
2. *Strategies for Alleviating Poverty in Rural Asia*, ed. Rizwanul Islam, Bangladesh Institute of Development Studies/ILO Asian Employment Programme, Bangkok, 1985, pp. 86 and 88.

# Chapter 9

1. Income Generating Activities for Refugees in Eastern and Central Sudan, 'The Revolving Fund Scheme', ILO/FRG/82/SUD/3, Terminal Report Phase 1, ILO, Geneva, 1989, p. 3.
2. Interview, November 1989.
3. Interview, December 1989.
4. Income Generating Activities for Refugees . . . 'The Revolving Fund Scheme', SUD/87/MOI/FRG, Progress Report July–December 1988, ILO, Geneva, p. 7.
5. Interview, December 1989.
6. Income Generating Activities of Refugees . . . 'The Revolving Fund Scheme', SUD/87/MOI/FRG, Progress Report January–June 1988, ILO, Geneva, p. 11.

# Chapter 10

1. Organization for Economic Cooperation and Development, *Financial Assistance for Developing Countries: 1988 and Recent Trends*, OECD, Paris, 1989.
2. Ozay Mehmet, *An Alternative to the Existing Multilateral Aid Delivery Systems: Learning from the NGOs*, University of Ottawa, 1981.
3. Quoted in *Doing Development*, ed. Richard Holloway, Earthscan Publications, 1989, p. 216.
4. Letter to author, January 1990.
5. Conversation with author, March 1990.
6. *British Overseas Aid: Anniversary Review 1989*, ODA, London, 1989, p. 83.
7. Holloway *op. cit.*, pp. 216–17.
8. Holloway *op. cit.*, p. 149.
9. Robin Poulton and Michael Harris, *Putting People First*, Macmillan, 1988, pp. 25–6.
10. Holloway *op. cit.*, p. 154–9.
11. *The AT Reader: Theory and Practice in Appropriate Technology*, ed. Marilyn Carr, IT Publications, 1985, p. 74.
12. Hansen *op. cit.*, p. 92.

# Chapter 11

1. Riddell *op. cit.*, p. 219.

# Bibliography

Berry, Albert (1989), *The Impact of Development Projects on Poverty*, Paris, OECD.

Carr, Marilyn (ed.) (1985), *The AT Reader: Theory and Practice in Appropriate Technology*, London, IT Publications.

Cassen, Robert (1986), *Does Aid Work?*, Oxford, Oxford University Press.

Chambers, R. (1983), *Rural Development*, Haslow, Longman.

Chr. Michelsen Institute (1986), *Bangladesh: Country Study and Norwegian Aid Review*, Bergen.

*Economist, The* (1990), 21 July.

Food and Agricultural Organization (FAO) (1987), *Agriculture: Toward 2000*, Rome, FAO.

Government of the Philippines, *1985 Census of Income and Expenditure*, Manila.

Griffith, Geoffrey (1987), *Missing the Poorest*, University of Sussex, Institute of Development Studies, discussion paper No. 23, May.

Hansen, Stein (1987), *India: Development and Aid, Norway's Contribution and Future Options*, Norway, Economic Research and Policy Planning.

Hart, Judith (1973), *Aid and Liberation*, London, Gollancz.

Hayter, T. and Watson, C. (1985), *Aid: Rhetoric and Reality*, London, Pluto Press.

HMSO, Cmd 6270 (1975), *Overseas Development, the Changing Emphasis in British Aid Policies: More Help for the Poorest*, London, HMSO.

Holloway, Richard (ed.) (1989), *Doing Development*, London, Earthscan Publications.

Howes, Michael, 1985, *Whose Water? An investigation of the consequences of alternative approaches to small-scale irrigation in Bangladesh*, Dhaka, Bangladesh Institute of Development Studies.

International Fund for Agricultural Development (IFAD) (1983), Annual Report 1982.

International Fund for Agricultural Development (IFAD) (1983), Project Document EB 83/19/R 42, Rome, IFAD.

International Fund for Agricultural Development (IFAD) (1984), Annual Report 1983.

International Fund for Agricultural Development (IFAD) (1984), 'Mid-term Evaluation Report of Bhima Command Area Develop ment Project', Rome, IFAD.

International Fund for Agricultural Development (IFAD) (1985), The Role of Rural Credit Projects in Reaching the Poor, IFAD Study Series, Vol. 1.

International Fund for Agricultural Development (IFAD) (1988), Annual Report 1987, Rome, IFAD.

International Fund for Agricultural Development (IFAD) (1989), Report on the Grameen Bank, EB 89/36/P 10/Rev.1, April.

International Labour Organization (ILO) (1989), Income Gener ating Activities for Refugees in Eastern and Central Sudan, 'The Revolving Fund Scheme', ILO/FRG/82/SUD/3, Terminal Re port Phase 1, Geneva, ILO.

International Labour Organization (ILO) (1988–9), Income Gen erating Activities for Refugees in Eastern and Central Sudan, 'The Revolving Fund Scheme', Progress Reports January–June and July–December 1988, Geneva, ILO.

IFPRI (1989), Irrigation Technology and Commercialization of Rice in the Gambia: Effects on Income and Nutrition, IFPRI Research Report, No. 75, Washington.

Islam, Rizwanul (ed.) (1985), Strategies for Alleviating Poverty in Rural Areas, Bangkok, Bangladesh Institute of Development Studies/ILO Asian Employment Programme.

Lecomte, Bernard J. (1986), Project Aid: Limitations and Alterna tives, Paris, OECD.

Marsh, D.K.V. and Dahal, R.P. (1984), Evaluation of the Small-Farmer Development Programme in the KHARDEP Area, Kath mandu, Agricultural Development Bank of Nepal, March.

Mehmet, Ozay (1981), An Alternative to the Existing Multilateral Aid Delivery Systems: Learning from the NGO, University of Ottawa.

Millwood, David and Gezelius, Helna (1985), Good Aid, Sweden, Swedish International Development Authority.

Mosley, Paul (1983), Can the Poor Benefit from Aid Projects?, Uni versity of Bath.

Mosley, Paul (1987), Poverty-focused Aid: The Lessons of Experience, London, Action Aid.

Nelson, Joan et al. (1989), Fragile Coalitions: The Politics of Econom ic Adjustment, Washington, ODC.

Organization for Economic Co-operation and Development (OECD) (1985), OECD Report, Paris, OECD.

Organization for Economic Co-operation and Development (OECD) (1989), Financial Assistance for Developing Countries: 1988 and Recent Trends, Paris, OECD.

Organization for Economic Co-operation and Development (OECD) (1989), OECD Aid Reviews, Paris, OECD.

Overseas Development Administration (ODA) (1989), *British Overseas Aid: Anniversary Review 1989*, London, ODA.

OXFAM (1989), Project Paper MPD 48,76,66, Oxford, OXFAM.

Pearson Report (1969), *Partners in Development*, London, Pall Mall Press.

Percy, Steve and Hall, Mike (1987), *British Aid to India. What Price?*, Nottingham, Spokesman Books.

Pleuris, John *et al.* (1988), *Strengthening the Poor: What Have We Learned?*, US–Third World Policy Perpectives, Washington, ODC.

Poulton, Robin and Harris, Michael (1988), *Putting People First*, London, Macmillan.

Population Reference Bureau Inc. (1989), *World Population Data Sheet*, Washington,

*Production, Processing and Marketing of Root Crops by Rural Women* (1988), Project Guidelines, Quezon City, Philippines, Agricultural Training Institute.

*Production, Processing and Marketing of Root Crops by Rural Women* (1990), Progress Report, October 1988–December 1989, Quezon City, Philippines, Agricultural Training Institute.

Report of the Independent Group on British Aid (1982), *Real Aid: A Strategy for Britain*, London, The Independent Group on British Aid.

Riddell, Roger C. (1987), *Foreign Aid Reconsidered*, Baltimore, John Hopkins/James Currey/ODI.

United Nations Children's Fund (UNICEF) (1984), Unicef, New York.

World Bank (1989), *1988 Annual Report*, Washington, The World Bank.

World Bank (1983), *World Development Report*, Washington, World Bank.